Thank You For Giving Me An Interesting *Life*

A Memoir of a Long, Slow, Loving Journey of Goodbye

Dr. Louis H. Falik

ISBN: 978-1-955531-20-7 (paperback)

Print information available on the last page.

DEDICATIONS

For Marilynn and Vera
For my life's prologue and epilogue, and the life in between.

To my son David
For sharing the difficult journey as his mother got farther and farther away.
We slowly lost a loving wife and beloved mother, together.

To Barry Peterson
For stimulating me to write of my journey through the sharing of his experience in his beautiful book Jan's Story. It encouraged and sustained me through the long goodbye from my Marilynn.

"In writing this book, Falik isn't afraid to describe all the thoughts and emotional that come with being a caregiver to a person summering through dementia…I appreciate that Falik begins his story before Marilynn had dementia since I feel that society tends to just see the disability or disease before they acknowledge the individual. Be describing her life before dementia, Falik humanizes her."

-*Literary Titan Review*

CONTENTS

PREFACE

This is both a memoir and diary. Memoir because I find myself thinking almost constantly about the history of our more than 55 years together, and my place in it. At this moment in time, I have experienced fifty-four plus years of marriage with two years prior to meeting and courtship. And two years of a new life companion who has helped me to understand and accommodate my loss and recovery.

Diary because I also find myself thinking from day to day. This was a transition time for me as well as Marilynn. For 7 or 8 years, I have had no one to talk to about this, no one at an intimate level. After Marilynn passed away and having a new intimate companion who through her life experiences deeply understands the process I experienced the events of my life to this point of time have become meaningful for me. I want to convey them because I feel it can help many others who are living through relationships where significant partners are declining into dementia. I know that my experience was not unique. Each life experience is different, but there are many shared qualities. I also know that the reading I did while Marilynn was slipping inexorably into her condition helped me to identify and accept my situation. I hope this recounting of my experience will be similarly helpful for others. Perhaps it will open consideration of how to deal with the situations that occur, how does one see and plan for the future of our loved ones and our own? What routines are repeated and effective, what is similar or different from day to day, comparisons to experiences of the same that occurred yesterday, last week, or even a few years ago. Thinking of Marilynn and my lives together, for close to 60 years, with lives intertwined through our youth, middle age, and advanced years leads to enduring memories.

I began this recollection as Marilynn is in what appears to be the final stages of mental decline, into a state that might be Alzheimer's but could well be something else. She has now passed on, into a state that my religious background refers to "as of blessed memory."

Early in the progression, I had taken her to a neurologist but the results were inconclusive. It might be Alzheimer's but it could be Parkinson's, or something else. The diagnoses are uncertain. There is much that needs further observation.

The first part of what I have written was when we were still in Israel, and being her primary caregiver while also trying to continue my professional life as a member of the Feuerstein Institute in Jerusalem, to which both Marilynn and I have given the last more than 20 years of our lives. But at the outset of this writing was accomplished usually after I had given her dinner, put her to bed (usually at 6:30 or 7:00 PM), giving me long evenings to contemplate and write. Where have we been? Where is this going? Are there changes to be made? What should they be? In what setting should they be enacted? And what and why do I want to write?

I am a writer. Much of my professional work has been devoted to areas of mental development and helping others to overcome deficits. I have been a clinician, offering direct services, a professor of counseling psychology, a researcher into cognitive development, and now as a writer and collaborator with a team of scholars and practitioners implementing the seminal work of our mentor, Professor Reuven Feuerstein. But I am writing for myself as a kind of comforting and search for understanding, and to put into words the memories that this stage of Marilynn and my life that are welling up? But as my recollections became more and more articulated (in my private self) I came to another place. Surely many others who have experienced some variation of what I was going through. Perhaps I can convey to others that which I am experiencing. That is what I have been doing for others for many years, though writing books and papers, consulting with parents and families, and working directly with children and adults to overcome their difficulties. Thus this story is directed toward two different levels: the narrative of our life together, and a focus on the issues of living with and dealing with a loved one experiencing a process of dementia. Concerning the second level, and my scholarly writing style, some of the language may seem academic. I hope it does not get too abstract. And perhaps because Marilynn has been a partner in all of this for so many years I may have difficulty separating the emotional from the technical.

As I write, I am conscious of the potential pitfalls throughout. But no matter, when I began I didn't need to consider these distinctions, only later when my goals for this memoir broadened. Early on in my recollections, my inclination was just to let it flow. I wanted to tell a story. But toward the end of this particular journey, after Marilynn passed away, approximately a year ago at the time of this writing, I more strongly feel that much of what I did, thought about, and now reflect upon has the potential to help others facing similar circumstances. This explains my "diversions" into explanatory concepts.

Another important influence for this writing stems from having been given a small book by a close friend who has observed Marilynn's decline and my reactions to it. It is called Jan's Story, by Barry Peterson. It is his first person account of his beloved wife Jan's descent into early onset Alzheimer's disease. I will describe and credit its role in my process as I unfold the narrative of Marilynn's descent into dementia. In fact, I attribute it as several places in this story. It contributed to my inspiration to write something that could be of help to others. To share my life with Marilynn in a way that gives a perspective on our experience, unique in some ways and commonly experienced in others. A perspective of mine, as a psychologist and helping professional, and hers—indirectly through the life we have lived together, her descent from high functioning toward mental decline. Some of the details will be elaborated as the story unfolds. But for the reader, this is a first picture of where we will go, and the progression of Marilynn's decline.

We have shared more than raising children, having embarked on similar career paths, and sharing in vocational activities—running a private school, working with children and adults, learning new and engaging ways of thinking, and working with people. So it is difficult to separate it all day to day, moment to moment. It is a story of collaboration, a shared love of our family and—most of all—a sense of adventure.

Here is a small window into the process that underlies this story, and how I have come to write it. I wrote some of the first pages while we were sitting in a training room in Taipei, Taiwan. Marilynn is sitting next to me as I train teachers to use the Feuerstein Instrumental Enrichment program. We were completing a one-month trip to 5 places in the

Far East—several places in India, Sri Lanka, and now Taiwan. Some training of teachers and psychologists, a few scholarly presentations at conferences, and some consultation with families who have disabled members for whom they hope that the cognitive modifiability practices of Feuerstein will help overcome the disabilities.

Marilynn wanted to be present in these encounters. She focuses and participates, mostly relevantly and coherently, although this is waning—less and less focus, increased restlessness, more rapid onset of fatigue. For this series of trips, I have made arrangements for an onsite caregiver who can sit with her, take her back to our hotel room when her attention starts to wander and she shows signs of restlessness. I also arranged for a family friend who has been a companion on previous trips to meet us in India and accompany us on several of the more demanding legs of the itinerary. But at this stage, being part of the training experience brings her back to her 30 years of learning the method, and many experiences teaching, training, and providing learning therapy to adults and children.

These things were all in a process of change, slowly and over several years. As the "symptoms" of her decline became more distinct I knew that decisions had to be made, and the nature of her decline started to activate me, chipping away at my denial, which I will address later in this narrative. I decided to consult with a social worker who specialized in this area of decision-making. I did so, and it was the beginning of focused planning.

Thus began the active focus, and acceptance of Marilynn's condition. With planning came awareness, and then contemplation. As her condition was slow-moving, and we had an active life around us, there was time and opportunity to understand and act.

This is the story of our life, how I and we reacted. I am ready to tell our story!

PROLOGUE

Jerusalem
2016

There is a farewell gathering for Marilynn, surrounded by our Israeli family and working friends. We are preparing to return to the US, as I have decided that I can no longer be Marilynn's caretaker. It is time to put her in care, and it was decided that the US was the best place, close to her children and grandchildren. It took me several years to come to this decision and represented a reality that I could no longer deny. She was loving and compliant, but no longer knew where she was, no longer able to initiate conversations (with a wonderful exception that will be told later in this story), but was starting to be resistant to my caregiving (another story that awaits telling later as well). I felt myself losing patience and on the verge of acting contrary to my sense of myself, and becoming angry and responsive to her emotional outbursts by saying or doing things that made me ashamed of my reactions and confirming my sense that I could no longer be her primary caregiver. It was time to make a change and we would return to the US.

The event was lovely. A gathering of 30 or 40 people. A sumptuous catered meal, and good feelings all around us. After the eating, we all sat in a large circle, and Rabbi Rafi Feuerstein, our host. and long-time colleague, and "family" friend, began to speak. He thanked us for our time in Israel, our work and commitment to people, and for contributing to the vision and impetus of his father, our loving mentor Professor Reuven Feuerstein. Marilynn was sitting on the other side of the room, holding the hand of his beloved wife Tal. As Rafi spoke, Marilynn became alive, and begin to respond to him, as though they were engaged in a dialogue. She was talking to him, and was cogent and aware. Given her state of withdrawal, it was remarkable.

After a few moments, she got up from her place with Tal and moved to sit closer to Rafi and continued to respond to his descriptions of our activities with our work and our relationships with the loving families who had "adopted" us in our lives in Israel. She was aware and connected to the situation and surroundings.

When the evening ended, we drove thirty minutes back to our apartment. As usual, she was sitting in the back of the car as I drove. After a few minutes of her usual silence, she said in a loud and clear voice "Thank you." I asked what she was thanking me for she responded, "Thank you for giving me an interesting life. I like my life. I am important. People love me!" That was it! Silent for the rest of the drive. Not responding to my questions might have drawn her out and helped her to elaborate on what she was feeling. And the next morning, it was gone.

In the following days, I wondered about what she said. I knew that there were moments of lucidity in the process of dementia that she was experiencing. I particularly wondered about the phrase "an interesting life." After several days of ruminating, I recalled something from our long life together. Two thoughts emerged: she often said that when we married she "knew" that we would have an "interesting life;" and with that recognition that she shared, and as we traveled around the world together doing the Feuerstein work and visiting unique and wonderful places…the Great Wall of China, the promontory at the very tip of Africa gazing down at the Atlantic Ocean and the Indian Ocean in our purview, watching sheepdogs work the flocks of sheep in New Zealand, climbing through the caves of Elephanta Island in the inland waterway of Mumbai, or sitting at sunset in a game lodge in the Masai range in Kenya watching animals approaching a water hole and drinking, one giraffe standing guard while the others drank—and so many others. I recalled the many times during those shared experiences we would turn to each other and say… "Aren't we having an interesting life." And then later, as I continued to think about the significance of the phrase, and how it emerged from the fog of her dementia was how she often said, throughout our marriage how that when we married she "knew she would have an interesting life."

Soon after we returned to the US and Marilynn was placed in care, and settled comfortably into this next, and last phase of her life. The event just described was both comforting and sad! The end was in sight. Who knew how long it would take and the course of subsequent events. But somehow comforting, as beneath the withdrawal was a deep sense of the satisfaction from the loving, interesting, and engaged life we had shared. Perhaps she was not completely gone!

The precise onset of her dementia was difficult to pinpoint. But by 2011 it was clear. At a training conference, she would leave a seminar room and not know how to return. She became incontinent. She was still socially responsive, but clearly less aware of where she was and what was happening around her. There had been a clue a year earlier. On a cruise with our immediate family, children, and grand-children, celebrating our 50th anniversary, she was able to participate in all the activities but seemed not to understand the reason for our celebration.

To me, these events, first in 2010 and then more clearly in 2011 did not disable our relationship. Others who have known us both over the years had observed her mental decline, for many more than three years. Family and friends who had not seen her for a long time often recalled events that I was aware of at the time but did not frame as mental decline. To me it was "just Marilynn, "she has been like this almost forever," and "we can deal with it, live with it, adjust to it." And so I made comfortable accommodations. But when it became clear, and the doctors did a CT scan, and I learned that her brain mass was at least 25% diminished, I could no longer engage in my mild and adaptive denial.

She became "of blessed memory" in April of 2019. She did not suffer until close to the end, or at least could not communicate her discomfort directly. At best, in the earlier stages of her dementia, she could not comprehend where she was and what she was experiencing, except perhaps at some deeper existential level. But I believe that the story of her and my life with her determined much of the ending. And that is the story to be told. Hopefully, it will illuminate meaningful aspects of the pathways one experiences along the way.
Now for the details of the journey we shared.

1

Our Beginnings

Ann Arbor, Michigan
1958

OUR FIRST MEETING

In my memory, the scene is bathed in the clear bright sunshine of a mid-September day. The excitement and energy are pervasive on the campus of the University of Michigan. It is orientation week, and I am there as a transfer student getting ready for my junior year. I had been at Eastern Michigan University, just down the road from Ann Arbor. I had not expected to survive in college, being a low average high school student, with undetected learning difficulties from early elementary school. But here I was, having done surprisingly well in my first two years, and ready for the heady academic atmosphere of the big, renowned, U of M. People were moving around central campus, looking at the buildings, meeting one another. Parents and their student offspring, students with students, and people like me just wandering around getting my bearings and wondering what my new life was going to be like.

It was in this golden moment of discovery that I met Marilynn. I had gone over to look at the Woman's League. In that time, and until today, the campus had a Men's Union and a Woman's League, institutions and their buildings from a time of the rigid segregation of the genders, but with their original purposes blurred. But it is the late 1950's and much of campus life, especially residentially, retained the gender separation. Men's and women's dormitories, fraternities and sororities, and the like. But here, I was outside of the Woman's League, wondering what it was, and I saw Marilynn for the first time. She was an entering freshman, on campus for the first time. I later learned that she had been accepted at Northwestern, in the Chicago area near where she lived, but made a last-minute decision to attend Michigan. One of the small decisions that come to affect the rest of our lives.

She was with my first high school girlfriend, Elaine. We greeted one another, and Elaine introduced me to Marilynn. They were to be room-mates in Mary Markley Hall, a newly built woman's dorm. We made small talk, and I found Marilynn to be very attractive. She was tall, very blonde, and carried herself with a quiet poise. Later I was to learn that her blonde hair was a "mistake." She had tried to lighten her natural chestnut-colored hair and it had "gone too far." But loved it, and thought her to be quite beautiful. Even later I learned that she did not consider herself as physically attractive as she was, in my eyes and I'm sure in the eyes of others. Later I learned that she thought her shoulders were too broad, her legs not thin enough, but she treasured her narrow waist. I considered her to be Rubenesque in form and stature, or more precisely, "Rubenesque-lite." She never accepted my allusions in this regard!

GETTING TO KNOW ONE ANOTHER

I asked whether she would like to meet me for a "coffee." She said yes, so we made a date. Neither of us was coffee drinkers and remained that way for the rest of our very long relationship, but that was what such meetings were called. In the climate of the university, such meetings were informal, frequent, and opportunities to get to know one another. Relating to "coffee," we were married for 5 years before Marilynn made a pot of coffee, and that was to be a good host for our friends "the coffee drinkers."

And so we met, and then met again. Slowly I decided that I liked her enough to gradually stop seeing the two or three other girls I was dating. We liked the same things and had very similar family experiences. We walked into the university's arboretum, went to the cinema, met for coffee and ice cream, and got to know one another. I recall that we talked about our families, our friends, our goals in life, as young university students are wont to do. She was 17 at the time and I was 20.

MAKING A RELATIONSHIP

An important part of this very early phase in our relationship was our "study dates." The U of M was academically very demanding. I had learned to survive and overcome my lackluster high school career, and relatively hidden learning disabilities by becoming a compulsive studier, forcing myself to spend at least 4 hours every evening. Marilynn joined me most evenings, as she was finding her academic load demanding. The university had just opened the Undergraduate Library (nicknamed the UGLY), and it became a site for a large number of students to gather, either singly or in pairs for evening study activities. So we worked on our assignments side by side, giving one another moral and logistical support. And going to and from was an opportunity to have a snack, get an ice cream cone, and walk and talk. During the day, we would coordinate our schedules to meet between classes on the "Diag," that was the communal intersecting space connecting several of the buildings where classes were held. A big, open place where students met one another between classes.

During that first semester, Marilynn confided that she was having particular difficulty in one of her classes, cultural anthropology. The format was several hundred students sitting in a large lecture hall listening to the professor, and taking notes. This was the primary class format for entering freshmen completing their liberal studies requirements. Once or twice a week the group was broken up into discussion groups, led by graduate assistants. In these smaller groups, the content was elaborated and clarified, and small quizzes were given, preparatory to larger mid-semester and final exams. She confided that her difficulty was that she was having trouble concentrating ("the professor looks like a great ape, going back and forth across the stage, swinging his arms back and forth while he talks"). She complained that she was so distracted by his physical appearance that she was not able to take cogent notes. She was so engrossed in his movements that she felt she was not listening or recording the content of what he was saying. I found her reaction fascinating, and wanted to see for myself what she was experiencing. I did not have a class at the time of the lectures, so I volunteered to attend with her, and take notes for her. I did so, and for the rest of the semester we attended the lectures together. During our "study dates" I would give her my notes and we would talk about the content. She passed the class—I don't recall with what grade—and we both learned anthropology together. This anecdote serves as a metaphor for the rest of our lives together, and the story to be told, as throughout our married lives we shared learning experiences and professional activities. I now look back on this early experience as a marker for our future.

We started going to Chicago together during our breaks. It was my first time in Chicago. I met her family and felt immediately comfortable with her parents and siblings, her sister and brother. Later in our life, they became important parts of our family configuration, socially and within the larger family system. We explored Chicago together, sharing what for me was a new and exciting experience. We visited museums, walked along Lake Michigan, went to concerts. I also liked going downtown with her as she shopped for clothing in the upscale department stores, another new experience for me. I was her consultant and it was a time of sharing as we got to know one another. She wore clothing well and had good taste. Interestingly, after 50 years of marriage, she still had garments from those early shopping excursions. She had great difficulty parting with them. "They are so beautiful," she would say, and at times they still fit! I would jokingly refer to her as "a sub-clinical hoarder."

I also met and came to know her extended family, her grandparents who were the true patriarch and matriarch of her family, her aunts and uncles, and cousins. Marilynn was part of a large, warm, and engaged extended family. They liked spending time together, shared many meaningful moments, in great contrast to the family I came from, that was isolated and without close relationships with our extended family. Or so it seemed to me at the time. I think that this part of Marilynn and my early experience together cemented my feeling that this was the person I wanted to spend the rest of my life with.

Toward the end of the first year of her university experience, Marilynn began to feel stress from the academic demands. She hung into the situation but began to feel stress and delay finishing assignments, often waiting to the last minute that increased the stress. I sometimes helped her to complete her assignments. I could see the difficulty she was having, and wondered what was going to happen, only being mildly judgmental, but never confronted. I finished assignments early and rapidly, planned ahead, and was uncomfortable with her last-minute responses and the stress she experienced.

Then summer came. At the time I was heavily engaged in summer camping, having been a counselor at overnight camps in the northern part of Michigan. I had been engaged in summer camping from my early childhood. It was a central part of my life. So we were apart, and I have no recollection of how she spent her summer. She may have taken a few summer school classes. But I was away in the north woods, working with kids and enjoying the activities of a long-term summer camping experience with peers and children—coordinating the athletic program, engaging in lakeside activities with canoes, water skiing, sailing, coaching tennis, and the like. And working with children and my adolescent peers. I believe that those years for me, from the age of 6 until I met Marilynn, every summer (and often in the winter working on school holidays as part of a maintenance crew), contributed to much of what I became as an adult. I learned to work with others, solve relationship problems among peers and campers (who were away from their homes and families for 4 to 6 weeks), and take responsibility for people and programs. In short, to be a helping person, which is what I later became as a psychologist and university professor.

But this is an important part of Marilynn and my story and became one of the first compromises I made to build and sustain a relationship. Her parents agreed to bring her to visit me at camp, and I secured permission for her to stay for several nights, joining one of the older girls' groups. It was quite an investment on her parent's part, as the drive from Chicago to the northern tip of the lower peninsula of Michigan was a major trip, especially at a time before freeways! They stayed in the area and made a holiday of it. The relevance of this incident to the larger narrative is that she came and was part of the camp's routines for several days. It became clear to me that she did not have the enthusiasm that I did, and that if I wanted to have a long-term relationship with her, summer camping was not going to be a part of it. I had a decision to make. If I wanted to be with her, and we were going to make a life together, I was going to have to alter my life course. I did, and have not regretted it, notwithstanding the summer camp dreams I had in March and April of every year for many years after that decision.

A PARTING, BUT NOT REALLY...

We returned to university for our next year, her second year and my senior year. For her the stress and tension mounted. She was not happy and found classes and requirements very difficult. We spent more and more time together, I supported her as much as I could, and in the face of her leaving me, we decided that we wanted to be married. We were committed to one another. She decided to not continue at the U of M, but return home to Chicago and enroll in Roosevelt University in downtown Chicago to finish her second year.

I stayed in Ann Arbor for my senior semester and then did summer school to finish some requirements for my teacher's credential, which had been a last-minute decision. There were frequent visits to Chicago. She came once to Ann Arbor to be with me. I also applied to graduate school, with the plan that we would live in Detroit where I could study with some desired professors at Wayne State University, and I could work as a substitute teacher in the Detroit schools to make our living as a married couple. And wedding plans were made. Marilynn didn't like my distance from the planning, as I generally wanted and agreed to whatever she wanted.

During the first semester, we drove to Chicago to announce to her family our desire to marry and get their blessing. I still have vivid memories of going to a restaurant with her parents, meeting her grandparents, and their love for her, acceptance of me, and our decision. Thus a wedding was planned for the following August. Much later, after Marilynn had deteriorated into her dementia, I came across correspondence that she had acquired from her mother relating to that early period of our engagement and the first years of our marriage. Included were letters exchanged between her parents and mine, who were getting to know each other, and who were sharing their feelings about our intended marriage. I read with tears in my eyes how our parents expressed their positive feelings about each of us, and how they were confident that we would have a long and happy life together. Significant in this shared communication was Marilynn's parent's concern that she would finish her education, and that our marriage would not interfere with this achievement. Later in this story, I will recount how assiduous Marilynn was in doing this, overcoming major obstacles, gaining her BA degree and teacher's credentials, and securing a position as an elementary school teacher. I recall now how Marilynn's mother, having observed this accomplishment, and knowing what Marilynn had to overcome to do it, said that after this she knew that we would follow up on the important things in life.

DECIDING TO SPEND A LIFE TOGETHER

Where to put my observations of Marilynn at the early time of our developing relationship? Perhaps this is a good place as any. When I met Marilynn, we began to spend time together; I was attracted to her personality, as well as her physical being. What did

I see in the former? She was quiet, somewhat shy in interpersonal interactions, in some ways projecting vulnerability, but beneath that veneer, a person having a strong inner sense of self, and a clear value system—she knew just what she wanted and didn't want. She did not always express it directly or immediately, and as we got to know one another, over a relatively short period, she seemed to enjoy my conveying externally her sense of herself to the world. Sort of like my "Aaron" to her "Moses." And I liked that role. I had to anticipate, articulate, watch for her subtle reactions, and then sensitively react. Too open or overt and she would withdraw, take it back, resist. (This was a quality of her reaction in the early phases of her dementia.) In some ways it reminded me of my interactions with my mother as I grew up, who had several of these qualities, but not too much! But with the right level of sensitivity and accurate reading of the situation, we became attuned, gave one another a sense of pleasure and accomplishment, and moved on to the next adventure. Often unspoken, but intimately understood. Eventually I came to see this as a kind of enabling. But I will elaborate on this part of our story later.

2

Our Early Years

Detroit, Michigan
1960

THE DECISION TO GET MARRIED

We were married in Chicago in August of 1960. We had known each other for slightly less than two years. Parenthetically, I hope it is not too irreverent to confess that in our generation at the time, and particularly in our cultural and family contexts, we respected greatly. If we wanted to be physically intimate (which we did), we both felt we should be married. We were almost the last of that generation, as many in our peer group were pairing off and getting engaged and married. I often reflected that if we had met a few years later, we would likely have moved in together and met our physical and relationship needs. I often wondered whether our lives might have taken a different turn if we had lived together and experienced one another's differences in living habits—her, not putting things away or in order, while I want everything in its place and organized. But I had no regrets, and I don't think she did either. However, I made lots of compromises during the first years of our marriage, with my enabling being primarily for my peace of mind.

THE DETAILS OF BUILDING A LIFE

We moved into a lovely duplex apartment and set up a house. We acquired a cat and extended our domestic life connecting with family and friends. I began a Master's degree program in psychology, and she enrolled in the same university to finish her BA. But she encountered difficulties from the outset. Her previous credits were not accepted, the university required onerous pre-requisites that meant that she would have to repeat much of what she had done at U of M and Roosevelt the previous year. The pathways to solution seemed impenetrable and frustrating. Some of the old tensions and anxiety returned. We decided that she should withdraw and seek other avenues.

We supported ourselves, living frugally, by my becoming a substitute teacher in the Detroit Public Schools and getting some help from her parents. It was a large district, and there was no shortage of assignments. It enabled me to take my university classes in the late afternoon and evenings, and not work when I felt overwhelmed with academic assignments. It also opened me to issues of education that became an important part of my later professional life.

In the second year of our marriage, I accepted a position with a university-related research project that required us to leave Detroit and take up residence in the small town of Coldwater, Michigan, in the center of the state. It was the site of an institution for the mentally handicapped (Michigan had several very large "homes" for the retarded, with populations of many thousands of wards) that was the site of the research project. The position required that we move periodically, every several months, to other similar institutions to research on a statewide basis. Coldwater was more than 50 miles from a satellite campus of the University of Michigan, in the city of Flint.

Marilynn applied for admission, and her previous undergraduate credits were accepted. She began driving three times each week from our first place of residence to the Flint campus and resumed her educational career. I marveled at her independence and focus, as driving a distance of 50 to 100 miles, through the Michigan winters took courage and an adventurous spirit. Later that year, we moved from Coldwater to

Lapeer, closer to Detroit, and a bit closer to her Flint campus. In both places, we set up housekeeping, and accustomed ourselves to small-town living, having been "big city" people all our lives. Again, Marilynn was accepting and accommodating. And she responded to the academic demands with confidence and success.

When I decided to leave the research project and take a position as a school psychologist in Dearborn, Michigan we moved house again, this time back into Detroit. Marilynn was able to transfer from the University of Michigan's Flint campus to their Dearborn campus, where she completed the remainder of her BA and graduated. With the teaching credential, she achieved she obtained a position as an elementary school teacher, in the second grade. She loved it, and from all appearances was an excellent, well-loved, and engaged teacher, with her students and their families.

When we became engaged her parents worried that she would not finish school. They remember—I do not—that I promised them that she would finish, and when she did, with all of the difficulties that she overcame, that cemented their respect for me and believed that we could accomplish anything we would set out to do in our lives. In retrospect, that was an accurate conclusion!

EVENTS OF FAMILY AND CAREER

After a year of living in another rented duplex apartment, we decided to buy a house. It was a risk, as we had little disposable income, and could not predict what the next years would be like for us, she a beginning elementary school teacher, and I in the early stages of my doctoral studies. But our nesting instincts prevailed and we took great pleasure in owning our own home and furnishing it. We ended up living in that house for only 4 years. Marilynn became pregnant with our first child, Alan, and wanted to stay at home and be a full-time mother. Her teaching career was thus limited to one year.

This was a time of child-rearing, and the activities of young married families with children. We had a small circle of friends, did the usual shared social activities with our children and as couples— theater, fairs and outings, and the like. First, my work in the Dearborn schools gave us a new set of friends, some of whom have remained so for the rest of our lives. The university where I had embarked on a Master's Degree began to offer some employment opportunities, so I shifted away from the Dearborn position and into full-time doctoral and research project activities. My recollections of those years center on our shared experiences as parents and through the social connections, Marilynn and I had through my various working situations.

Upon completing my Doctorate, we decided to move to California when I accepted a position at San Francisco State University. So time to move again and set up a house in a new and unfamiliar environment. Part of the allure of accepting that move was that we would be closer to Marilynn's family who had moved to California several years earlier and that we had visited San Francisco as tourists a few years earlier and found it to be a most beautiful and attractive place to live.

We wondered how long we would be there, as in the academic world that I was entering faculty tended to move to new positions every 4 or 5 years—in the mid-1960's university programs were expanding and moving to a new position was the route to advancement. We were ready for anything!

We had decided to wait a few years before having children. Alan came in the fourth year of our marriage. Alan was 2 years old when we moved to San Francisco. At the time of our move, Marilynn was pregnant with our second son, David, who was born in California. Marilynn loved being pregnant and was healthy and vigorous throughout. There is a photo of her raising the mainsail on the small sailboat we had, in the 8th month of her first pregnancy. A sense of adventure, perhaps a bit risky, but we were young!

We both were excited at the prospect of parenthood and loved being parents to our beloved Alan, and then two and a half years later our David. But life has lots of small crises that must be overcome. Alan was born at less than 5 pounds, and the hospital required him to stay in the neonatal nursery until he gained some weight, so Marilynn had to come home without him. But after a few days, we brought him home and began the new phase of our lives as parents. Just after David's birth an ovarian cyst was discovered and Marilynn needed surgery.

Alan was easy to care for as an infant, but as he gained mobility was quite active. We had started with the son of the pediatrician that had cared for me and my siblings. When he prescribed phenobarbital for Alan's "presumptive" hyperactivity Marilynn adamantly held that she was not going to have her son "drugged," and we had to find a new doctor. We did so, and Marilynn accepted and dealt with his activity levels. I recall talking to her on the telephone from my work and her saying "I am following him around the house, putting things back into closets and cupboards that he has taken out, and when we get to one end of the house we start over again." We talked about this and decided to be proud of Alan's exploring his environment and its plethora of sounds, textures, shapes, and the social interaction (Marilynn following him) involved. Alan was not much of a daytime sleeper, and Marilynn found that if she drove him in the car he would sleep, awaking as soon as she pulled into the driveway of our house and turned off the engine. In retrospect, at this writing, I realize that she (and I) had a sense of the developmental and cognitive needs of the young child, something that came to professional fruition for both of us much later in our lives. And that we talked about it, shared in our growing understanding, and loved the situation we were in!

When it came time to make our move to California, we sold our house, made decisions about what furniture we would send to California, and arranged the details. Another instance of shared decision-making. At this point, further evidence of Marilynn's independence and adventurous spirit was shown. We decided that she would drive across the country ahead of me, as I had research project tasks and some teaching to complete. She took off with one of our cars, accompanied by my sister, and our almost two-year-old child. The journey from Detroit to San Francisco was complicated by Alan's activity level, and the prospect of keeping him in a car for the many hours of driving that was required. We decided that they would take their time, stopping often and not driving more than 5 or 6 hours in a day. We dealt with Alan's activity level by bringing his tricycle so they could stop from time to time and let him ride off his energy. Another complication was the fact that the interstate highway system was still in the process of completion, requiring numerous and lengthy detours. And of course, this was long before there was GPS to guide us. They did it, had a positive adventure, and got to San Francisco and began the process of settling in. I followed three weeks later in our other car, and arrived to a happy wife and child, positively anticipating our new life in California.

I provide these descriptive details because they remind me that Marilynn was a competent, goal-oriented, adventurous, and fully loving partner. We were in our 20's. Our lives were ahead of us.

We embraced the possibilities of our lives ahead. We excitedly and collaboratively planned our future. We took risks with the pleasurable anticipation of what was to come. Nothing that happened later diminished my pleasure in recalling this phase in our lives and in some ways sustained me in the events that followed many years later.

We lived in a rented town house for the first few months in California, but wanted our own home so as in Detroit we "took the risk" of buying a house, again with limited resources. We both exercised our "nesting instincts," buying furniture, planning our living environment, and enjoying the "California" open space, compared to our lives in Detroit and Chicago. It was a pleasant adventure for both of us.

I began my university career and Marilynn was mother to Alan and carrying our second child into the later stages of pregnancy and birth. She was an engaged mother, taking pleasure in the boys' growth, and melding into the suburban life of the community. As a young faculty member, we became involved in the social aspects of the university community, and she made friends with both our neighbors, their young children, and our university faculty comrades.

OUR PHYSICAL ATTRACTION TO ONE ANOTHER

An important part of our story, for this point in our lives and later, was our physicality. We were both very sexually attracted to one another, enjoying the closeness of holding one another, and constantly touching and caressing one another. But as a very young married couple, for both of us, this was our our first physically intimate relationship, we found ourselves exploring the possibilities and moving slowly, gently, and ultimately with satisfaction and comfort. This lasted throughout the entirety of our marriage, until the degree of dementia began to erode Marilynn's capacity to accept physical contact and understand and reciprocate the affection that had always been a mutually satisfying experience. As her dementia deepened this all changed, and for the last 5 years of her life we were not sexual. At first she seemed confused, uninterested, and a passive participant. Then the touching appeared to be painful. So we stopped having sex, but did not abandon the kissing and hugging, as long as it did not seem to be uncomfortable for her.

THE ACCOMMODATIONS OF A RELATIONSHIP

In the aftermath of Marilynn's mental deterioration, I have thought a great deal about the accommodations that I made, almost from the beginning. I have come to understand that in any functional relationship, wanted to be a good husband and great father requires a good deal of enabling (something I will elaborate on later in this story).

Here is an example: A good argument for living together before marital commitments are made, one of many, is that we never really know what our partner's living habits are until we live with them. Dating, and intimacy, and many shared experiences may not shed light on the day-to-day ways of living. I came from a family, expressed through my mother, where everything had to be in its place, and that to not put things away was akin to committing a mortal sin—if not that, then a great deal of discomfort, or it would be discarded (in my youth I retrieved many things from the trash if they had sat out for more than a day). When Marilynn and I set up our first connubial home, I discovered that she did not have the habit of putting things away, that piles of clothing were left in the corners of our rooms, that she had almost no system of order in the kitchen, and that what was unfamiliar domestic chaos for me did not bother her in the least. It was a serious contrast to my fastidious and compulsively ordered mother. But at the same time, I had grown up with a father who was a gentle and accepting, almost prototypical caregiver—he endeavored with every fiber of his being to accommodate to my mother. And she was not always pleasant about it. But with sweet gentleness he would do her bidding, and they developed—to my childhood eyes—a comfortable way of making a home. So I came to my living experience with Marilynn with this heritage. Things should be in their place (from my mother), there should be no conflict (from my father) was no conflict. But in my

first independent domestic experience, I had to come to terms with Marilynn's lack of attention to neatness and order. Or something like that--just take out your statement that this characteristic was from her family experience. I hope I am not sounding judgmental here, only descriptive. Luckily this contrast contributed to my accommodation tendencies. What did I inherit from my father? Ways to make it work, to suppress my annoyance, actually to reframe it to make things comfortable for me and Marilynn. And that is how we lived, through gradually larger domiciles, with the inevitable accumulation of material goods— clothing, furniture, jewelry, appliances, and the like.

MAKING IT WORK

In the large house in San Francisco that we lived in for close to 30 years, after 20 years of marriage, I just kept building more storage closets, and arranging new ways to store things to avoid the inevitable "black holes" of lost and forgotten stuff. This was brought home to me when we sold and moved out of our house, and had to deal with the accumulation of more than 40 years of "precious objects." By this point in time, Marilynn had already started her descent into dementia, although I don't think I knew it at the time. With humor, I labeled her as a "sub-clinical hoarder," as I saw—and knew—that she could not bear to get rid of almost anything. When we moved from our large and spacious home into a one-bedroom apartment, it was necessary to deal with the accumulation of clothing, books, papers, pots and pans, her spice collection, and other whatnots.

And I accommodated. We found outside storage, I made storage spaces in the apartment complex we were moving into (fortunately we owned the building so I could do it), and finally, I secretly began to dispose of things I knew she would not remember. But we had to keep dresses from the early days of our marriage, as each time I asked her for a decision she would reply, "Oh that is so beautiful, I am not giving it away..." and other such comments. At the very end, when she was long gone mentally, and I was giving to charity her extensive clothing wardrobe/collection, all this came flooding back for me.

Then more than 15 years later, and two more residential moves, well into Marilynn's dementia, I needed to dispose of so much of her "beloved" accumulation. This move was from our Jerusalem apartment into a two-room apartment in San Francisco. I still did it somewhat secretly, but that was as much from habit as she had no memory of her possessions, and a very limited scope of utility—in her closets, in the kitchen that she no longer operates within—the process of disposal was much easier. And back to my dynamics, from the big house to the smaller apartment, and from there into an even smaller living space, in these transmissions I got comfort from closets that were no longer jammed with unused objects, and I slowly created an order and accessibility in the several places that we lived. That brought me back to my early life and gave me a sense of comfort. But at the same time disposing of her last things made me sad.

3

Deepening the Ties

San Mateo-San Francisco
1960 to 1980

RESPONDING TO CHALLENGES

Thus we continued the process of building a family and making a career, fully shared for both of us. How to convey this part of contributing to Marilynn's "interesting life?" My recollections of these years are colored by a mist of contentment as we moved from our student days together into becoming a loving couple, and then into our shared parenthood. First in Detroit where I embarked on completing my Ph.D.,and then our "intended" the first move, to California where I took an academic position at San Francisco State University. It was a time of growing into our modified roles, exploring our shared values, and primarily of sharing—she with my academic world and I with her experiences as a young mother, as a supportive and fully contributing father. She showed great courage in her need to nurture Alan, who was born 4 years into our marriage, while I was still studying. For example, while still in Detroit, although she was never comfortable swimming, she took infant Alan to the YMCA and joined a program to make infants accustomed to being in the water, which meant that she had to be in the water with him. (Parenthetically, he became an early swimmer and was always comfortable in the water.) I knew it was hard for her, but she was dedicated. Another memory from a later time was when on a trip to Switzerland she hiked along narrow mountain passes, and slid down shafts of a salt mine sitting on mats, David on her lap and Alan on mine, suppressing her fears of the precipitous decline and speed of the trip. They never knew that she was extremely fearful of heights, narrow pathways.

These years were not without the usual stresses of life. First, we had very limited financial resources, and how to meet the needs of our young children. Then the frequent moves, the illnesses of children and extended family members, and my building my career. But each crisis is an opportunity, and that is how we responded. During these early years, there were no signs of any mental or emotional weakness. Quite the contrary!

Another potential stressor might have been my career issues. As a young faculty member attempting to secure his place in academia, with the teaching and research demands, and a tendency to get involved (some might say over-involved) in numerous activities related to (and supporting my goals), I was very engaged, affecting both time and focus. Marilynn shared in all of this, was encouraging, and seemed to be comfortable with her role as Alan's, and then soon after, David's mother.

Alan as two and a half year old was socially very outgoing. And he became aware that other children were attending "murthday" school as he labeled it. Of course, he was a bit too young, but I found that there were several short-term, practicum-oriented play-group programs at my university, and since the instructors were my colleagues and Alan was socially precocious, they accepted him, much to his joy. So I would take him and bring him home, and it was an adventure for both of us. My university schedule permitted it, and I was willing to do a lot of "coming and going" driving that this required.

And so we raised our young sons and built our family. One incident from that period stands out. In addition to my teaching and university activities, most of which were in the later afternoon and evenings, I was doing a good deal of consulting in the community and had joined a consultant group developing projects in other cities. So relatively rapidly I found myself traveling once a month to Denver, Seattle, St. Louis, and even Honolulu for several days of working with teachers and parents on various school improvement projects. During this time, we were having dinner together at home, and I looked up to see Alan with tears in his eyes. I asked him what was the matter, and he said "Oh, daddy, I am so glad you decided to come home and have dinner with us!"

After telling Alan that I too was happy to be able to have dinner with the family, and we put the boys to bed, Marilynn and I had a long talk. We decided that I would cut back on my "extra-curricular" activities for a few years. We did not want the boys to feel that they did not have a father. And as a family, we wanted to engage together in a wide range of wonderful adventures. For the next few years, including a major move from the suburb of San Mateo into the city of San Francisco, we did just that.

From the birth of Alan, and as David came, Marilynn wanted to stay at home and be a mother. As soon as the boys understood and were able, they wanted to be in pre-school, so we found programs for them. Usually, they were parent "co-operatives" that required mothers, and fathers, to participate. These programs required mothers in the classrooms and fathers to work on periodic details to uphold the physical surroundings. When Marilynn was scheduled to be in the classroom, and it was difficult for her (as the mother of infant David), I would occasionally pinch-hit for her. Since most of my university duties (teaching, meetings, supervision, and the like) were in the afternoons and evenings, I could do it. Also, since I was professionally interested in child development, learning development, interpersonal relationships, etc., it gave me a chance not only to be with Alan but also to observe more broadly processes of great interest to me.

OUR "FAMILY SYSTEM" DEVELOPS

What were these years like for Marilynn, and me? Many events shaped our experience during that time and set the pathway for our future. Our first California home was in San Mateo, a suburb of San Francisco. We lived there for six years. But our social life was centered in the city, and we began to feel like it would be nice to live closer to the university where I taught, and the various cultural activities we enjoyed—theater, symphony, museums, and the like. So we casually began looking at houses, and found something that was a dream. We found a large house, a few blocks from campus, in an upscale neighborhood, and at a price we could almost afford. So another risk-taking experience.

New schools for the boys, a more foggy climate than we were used to in San Mateo, and finding a new set of friends. For the first few weeks after the move, Marilynn had regrets. Had she really wanted to leave the life we had in the suburb? With the unfamiliar shopping and daily routines? And what about her friends? But as many times before, we adapted to the new, got back into the nesting routines of furnishing and settling, and learned to love our elegant new home. This process only took a few weeks! And the boys adjusted as well, with schools and friends. Marilynn made new friends, and we embarked on an active life. We lived in our new home almost 30 years.

One of the features of our new home was a bottom floor, accessible from the outside, with facilities for setting up private practice for me, and—later—an office for her where she could see children and adults for learning development assistance. (This part of the story requires some details that will be recounted in the next chapter.) So we finished empty space, remodeled, and built—first a playroom for the boys with a pool table and table tennis, and later the space for her work adjacent to my work space.

MOVING OUT INTO THE WORLD

As the boys got older, Marilynn was ready to relinquish her role as a stay-at-home mother. One of my activities at the time was to be involved in an after-school tutorial program for students with learning disabilities. This later morphed into a day school. As it made this transition, we needed someone to coordinate the after-school program, and Marilynn was interested. Although she had not had specific experience with learning disabilities, she took on the task. It required scheduling, monitoring the various tutors and their programs, meeting with parents and teachers, and dealing with the program directors, myself, and two of my co-directors. She had to commute from our home in San Francisco to the Peninsula, approximately 20 miles each way. She did this four days a week, often being out until early evening. Our boys were alternatively proud of their mother and complaining that she was not there to greet them at the end of their school days or extra-curricular activities. I found time to take them to their activities and be a support for them. I went to their soccer games and practices, took them to classes in the dramatic arts, science museums, and the like. When Marilynn could she did, but we had a comfortable sharing of these routines.

BECOMING A STUDENT AGAIN

Marilynn decided that she would like to get a Master's Degree in marriage and family counseling. That was one of my teaching areas at San Francisco State University, which now happened to be just 6 blocks from our home. But she could not do it there, as she was socially involved with many of the faculty, and my role in the program. The logistics would have been so easy, but here was another of the obstacles in life to overcome! There was a program at California State University, Hayward, approximately 50 miles away and on the other side of the Bay. She applied and was accepted, but had to take almost a year of pre-requisites to be admitted. She took this on, as she had done years earlier to complete her undergraduate degree, and so began a three year commute, a graduate program of academic studies, often driving at night to return from evening classes requiring crossing bridges and engaging in rush hour traffic (before cell phones and GPS were available to guide her or communicate when she was stuck or in difficulty).

She did well in her classes, and enjoyed the academic and social contacts. Writing papers was never easy for her, and from time to time I helped her, just like our university days. Putting her ideas into formal words and grammatical structures was difficult as she tended to block her expression of what she wanted to say. In talking with her about a project, she knew what she wanted to say, but could not get it out with fluency or comfort. In addition she was a very poor typist, and the typewriters at the time (late 1970's, early 1980's, manual or electronic) made it even harder to compose and produce text—think of the physical effort of guiding one's fingers even with "touch typing" skills, of

correcting errors, starting over from page to page, and the like. But the first Apple Macintosh computers were coming on the market, with all the hype about how much easier they were to use. Feeling that this might alleviate some of this particular stress, I bought her one. It did the trick, sort of, at the level of physical effort involved, the ability to correct errors, the capacity to "cut and paste" content from one place to another in the text all conspired to ease up some of her "writer's block." Nevertheless, from time to time, in moments of "last minute performance anxiety" (recalling her undergraduate study habits I've described earlier) I would volunteer to type something out for her. It helped her out and gave me opportunity to learn how to word-process on the computer. When she had completed the writing for her classes and her MA thesis, I took the computer "away" from her to try it out on my work (transitioning away from my manual typewriter for report writing, scholarly papers, and the like) and never gave it back. What an improvement over composing on the typewriter! Even though her needs for writing almost completely vanished, it was a source of good natured recrimination between us… "You took my computer away from me and never gave it back!"

A major problem occurred at the end of her degree process. Her program required a thesis paper as the culminating experience. Given what is described just above, it was a major source of difficulty— formulating a proposal, doing the research, and writing the thesis. This was done under the supervision and presumed guidance of an assigned faculty advisor. As the process unfolded and Marilynn selected a topic and began the work, the faculty advisor who had worked with her and approved the project changed his mind, without much rationale at least from her perspective, and told her to start over with a different topic. Marilynn was devastated, and became anxious, angry, and blocked (not being a comfortable writer, to begin with). She became so blocked that I feared for her mental state, and the potential loss of all that she had accomplished. I asked her if she wanted me to intervene since I knew the faculty and the program she was in (but not the particular faculty member who was the source of her conflict). She agreed, and we made an appointment with the department chairman (who was a colleague of mine in the "politics" of counselor education at the statewide level) to discuss the situation, and the injustice of it for Marilynn, who had already done a great deal of work on the rejected topic. A compromise was reached, Marilynn was assigned a new thesis advisor who

was deemed easier for her to work with, and the situation was resolved.

I felt that she had been badly served, perhaps because she was not as assertive with the first thesis advisor, but I did not make an issue of it. As I think about this incident, it seems to me to be another of my "positive" enabling actions that characterized our relationship. My rationale came from two directions: Marilynn had successful and productive relationships with all of her other faculty instructors, was highly motivated to finish her program and become a marriage and family counselor, and I knew enough about the program she was in, and the various faculty members, to feel that she was the victim of an unjust process by an insensitive faculty member. It was also clear that she could not have resolved the situation on her own.

She went on to complete her fieldwork requirements in a family service agency, developed a thesis topic from her fieldwork, and both enjoyed the confidence of her field supervisors and completed her thesis with her new thesis advisor. She received her MA degree and was "ready" to move on to the next stage of the process, accumulating internship hours toward gaining her California MFT license. This was a source of anticipatory anxiety, particularly the test she would have to take at the end of the process, but fate intervened.

4

Widening the Scope of the Journey

San Francisco-Jerusalem-and Beyond
1990-2010

SOME EARLY SUBTLE SIGNS, AND RESPONSES

The story continues in a positive vein, but with some of the first gentle signs of diminished capacity evident, that I didn't recognize or have concerns about at the time. But here I must take the reader on a slightly academic diversion.

I used a term at the end of the last chapter that in subsequent years I have thought a great deal about. I know myself to be an "enabler." Our relationship as loving partners endured and flourished through the adjustments and compromises that were made on all manner of issues. That is enabling, but of a very different sort than is usually described in the mental health field. This insight comes from my ruminating about my life with Marilynn, especially as she began to show signs of her mental decline. But I was also a practicing psychologist and university professor, actively teaching in the earlier stages of this story, and in an active "retirement" up to the writing of this memoir. So concepts such as I am about to elaborate are relevant and expected, given who I am and my life with Marilynn.

POSITIVE ENABLING

I accept the label of enabler without any sense of guilt or apology. I suspect it is embedded in my family history, and certainly reflected in the professional career I have chosen. I consider this to be one of my better personal characteristics. I am a "caregiver," have been from the earliest days of my memory, in my family (not an infrequent response as the oldest of three siblings), in my peer group, and through several years as a summer camp counselor in my later adolescence. Not coincidently I have developed my professional life in accordance with these characteristics.

But the long-term experiences in my relationship with Marilynn, along with the other characteristics I have described have caused me to think deeply about the concept of enabling. Reflecting on my experience as a psychologist and professor in the mental health training field, I have come to see the concept of enabling quite differently.

In recent years the term "enabler" has acquired a negative connotation. It is usually associated with how those in relationships deal with their partners when issues of alcoholism, drug addition, domestic violence, and other such maladies of modern life are experienced. The implication is that in such conditions, there is someone who reacts in such a way as to sustain the condition, eventually preserving the status quo, for a variety of reasons—out of a desire to avoid conflict, provide hope for safety, or fear of confrontation. In this context, enabling occurs either by direct and conscious actions or by inadvertent and non-conscious actions to meet the needs of the enabler. (For me it was both.) For example, in the mental health field spouses who are victims of domestic violence continue to return to their partners, denying the possibilities of recurrence and rationalizing their decisions, thereby enabling a furtherance of the domestic violence. The dynamic is unfortunately similar in addictive behavior situations. And so dysfunctional relationships continue, usually to the detriment of all parties involved.

As I write this I sense I may have some serious convincing to do, as the negativity of the concept is well engrained in our social concepts. But I am increasingly convinced that my life with Marilynn was a testament to the potential for a positive reframe of what it means to be an enabler. And I strongly suspect that I am not alone. I also believe that positive enabling is associated with shared and comfortable compromising, stabilizing relationships, and making it possible to move on in mutually satisfying ways. Yes, there is a need system involved. But the needs can be viewed in accordance with life-affirming and adaptive motivations.

As I have contemplated my long life with Marilynn and connected it to my family of origin upbringing, I have worked out a "reframing" of what it means to be an enabler. Not surprisingly, given that I am recollecting my own life as well as hers, and I have a generally positive sense of myself (hopefully accurately), I believe I have been a positive enabler. I believe that this enabling caused us to live a productive life, being loving and sharing partners, and made the road toward her mental decline smoother, more extended, and eventually less stressful, for her as well as myself. Let me explain further.

This fits the operational definition of enabling. Everything that the negative enabler does to sustain the condition the positive enabler does for the same goals of sustaining. The same dynamic of conscious or non-conscious awareness obtains. The difference is in what is sustained! In the positive reframe, actions are taken, compromises constructed, and outcomes are those that create ongoing positive consequences. As I continue to tell the story of Marilynn and my relationship, these elements will emerge. That which might be potentially or ultimately disabling, or at least dysfunctional, is responded to optimistically and functionally, with structures, options, and modifications that create working and comfortable solutions.

RESPONDING TO THE SIGNS

Thus, for Marilynn and me, almost from the beginning, I have been an enabler. At first on small issues, like picking up her discarded clothing from the floor, or keeping her kitchen relatively organized, and the like. I was doing it as much for me, and my sense of comfort. We would often make a joke of her piling clothing in a corner of her room. I would lightly observe that "mount Marilynn" was getting high, and might need some "excavating." She would laugh, and then put "most" of her clothing back into closets and drawers. And when the closets and drawers became too chaotically packed, we would go on exploratory "snark hunts" to find something that she was unsuccessfully searching for, usually with good humor and a sense of shared adventure. Once in a while I would moralize—"this would not happen if you were better organized, etc."—but not too often. And Marilynn did not seem offended.

Examples of the more flagrant forms of my enabling of this behavioral characteristic extended to the kitchen as well as the bedroom. I built or expanded closets and storage places. Fortunately our house was big, had lots of potential places for structural changes, and I enjoyed the creative planning and carpentry it required. It didn't fully extinguish the behavior, but kept it under control, with my periodic interventions. And again, I was comfortable. Put another way, I dealt with my comfort needs without frequent moralizing, negative attributions, and Marilynn did not feel attacked or confronted, at least not too much!

Up until the later period of her decline, it continued to amaze me that despite of a chaotically organized kitchen, with little order to cooking utensils, ingredients, or the spice cabinets, she seemed to know where things were and was a wonderful cook and prolific baker, taking pride in this latter aspect of her culinary interests.

Later the adaptations that needed to be made were more serious, as her deterioration began to manifest itself, such as restricting and then prohibiting her driving when she began to get lost traversing familiar territory. Some of these details will be forthcoming as the story unfolds. For me, in the earlier stages of her process, we were encountering exciting, confirming, life-affirming encounters with an exciting world, and these characteristics seemed easy to deal with. And being relatively young, moving out into a very exciting world of professional and social activity the issues were not problematic.

There are three important differences however in the role of the "positive" enabler. First, the ability to gently say no, to propose workable alternatives, and to overtly convey what is self-enhancing and what is not. And secondly, more importantly, to have a positive sense of goals, directions, and mutual self-development. Finally, to act forthrightly im plementing the alternatives, and stay with them.

In later years, as I became a psychologist, and learned the skills of marriage and family counseling, I could differentiate those couples who had these attitudes and inclinations from and those who did not, and observe how they were reflected in their relationships. For myself, in my marriage and our shared parenting with Marilynn, I did most of those positive things just described without overt conscious intentionality, but as I look back over the more than 50 years of our being together, I can see clearly that I was acting within this framework. As I reflect on these issues as we got closer toward the years of her more distinct deterioration, I see how the unconscious part was the meeting of my needs and the underlying dynamics for me were tacting in consonance with my family history. That is what probably made it so comfortable. In further retrospect, it probably extended her cogent and productive mental life many years.

RECALIBRATING A CAREER

Earlier I referred to two events that shaped the next phase of our lives. One was Marilynn's completion of her MA degree and somewhat anxious contemplation of the hurdle of internship and finishing the licensing requirements to become a marriage and family therapist. A second, and ultimately more significant, was our increasing involvement in my activities relating to the learning theories and practices of Professor Reuven Feuerstein who was to become one of the eminent cognitive psychologists in the world. I began to travel to Israel, the site of his international institute, to learn, and eventually to become an active member of the international institutions that he created. In the first few years of this involvement our older son, Alan was living on a kibbutz and Marilynn would accompany me to Israel, to visit our son and participate in various training activities at the institute.

GAINING AND SUSTAINING COMPETENCE

Sitting in on numerous learning experiences, seminars, and consultation opportunities, we learned together. She was interested, it connected to her earlier experience as a teacher and coordinator of a program for students with learning disabilities. So for a period of five or six years, we made numerous trips to Israel, and got more and more involved in the activities of the Feuerstein Institute. But as she learned the Feuerstein techniques she wanted to apply them to children and adults, and she was a good teacher, mediator, and assessor of learning development. It pulled her away from her initial motivation to become a marriage and family therapist.

She began to accept referrals in San Francisco, emanating from her previous contacts in our school program that she had coordinated, and the growing reputation of the effectiveness of the Feuerstein approach. So sometimes she did not want to leave her clients and stayed at home when I went to Israel, usually for shorter trips. And as I began to travel abroad to offer Feuerstein training sometimes she accompanied me and sometimes not. This pattern was obtained for many years, from the late 1980s until well into 2015 when her level of dementia made it too difficult for her to continue. But when we were together in Israel or elsewhere, she was an active participant, involved, and knowledgeable.

Her level of skills developed such that in the earlier period that I am describing when Marilynn was in residence in Israel and at the Institute, Professor Feuerstein would give her difficult cases to work with. I can recall many instances of watching her work with children and adults, listening to the supervision she was getting from Professor Feuerstein, and our discussing her work together, mutually expanding our learning. I saw and tried to reinforce her sense of her competence.

When she did accompany me she related well to the details of the journey and made wonderful personal connections with those we worked with, students, parents, and hosts. One of the related experiences of these trips, particularly if we were in a location for an extended time (several weeks, or in a few instances a month or more), parents would come to us and ask us to evaluate and/or treat their children. I would see some children; Marilynn and I would evaluate them, then consult with the families, and in some instances would initiate some extended therapeutic or tutorial activities for the time period we were there.

In one such instance, we were in Australia for six months (I had a sabbatical leave from my university) and we worked with several very severely low functioning children. It was demanding work, and when we finished that experience I told Marilynn that the work she did with the children "made her an expert therapist!" And she gained a confidence that stayed with her until her cognitive capacities no longer enabled her to function.

DEEPENING OUR COMMITMENT TO A DIFFERENT PATH

For much of the 1990s and into the 2000's we spent more and more time in Israel, eventually buying an apartment in Jerusalem. Marilynn became an active member of the team of teachers and therapists at the institute, then called the International Center for the Enhancement of Learning Potential (ICELP). As we traveled together internationally she became known to our "Feuerstein" colleagues, and was valued as a participant in the learning and consulting processes. After she could no longer travel, and eventually passed away, people asked me about her and had tears in their eyes as I described her descent into incapacity. She was respected and much loved. Part of this was due to our being in training and consulting settings where we developed meaningful relationships with people (parents, children, teachers, etc.) that endured over many years.

We spent these years traveling back and forth between San Francisco and Israel, and increasingly to other places in the world where the Feuerstein programs were being disseminated. In the early years, I committed to teach at my university for one semester, as a requirement for early retirement, so that meant six months in San Francisco. Later, as my university requirements were completed, we would spend several months in one place or another. In the earlier years, before 2001, we did not have an apartment in Israel, so we were in the country as itinerants, sometimes in hotels, sometimes in apartments provided for us by the Institute. It required flexibility and willingness to adapt. Marilynn never complained, and we felt a sense of adventure as we got to know different parts of Jerusalem. For example, one hotel we stayed in several times was near the open-air market, referred to by the natives as the "shouk." Every morning we would walk through the market on our way to the Institute, buy fresh loaves of bread that had just been baked there, and other things for our lunch or dinner.

Again, this phase of our lives together was infused with a sense of adventure. Filled with new experiences, meeting new people, and widening our scope of both personal relationships and professional competencies. We both felt excited, confirmed, involved in meaningful and interesting activities. Hence a window into Marilynn's deep memory, pushing through her cognitive decline, of having "an interesting life."

5

The "Feuerstein" Years:

A Gradual Descent

Jerusalem-San Francisco

Globally
2001-2016

This chapter continues recounting the small details of our life. Why the details? Because as we lived the journey of Marilynn's gradual descent, especially in retrospect, the nuances of the details reflect levels of meaning—what could be termed the "back story." And in the effort to reconstruct the nature of our lives together, from the perspective of the long, slow, and subtle journey into Marilynn's dementia, it is ultimately the small, mundane details of our lives that reflect meaning.

A TIME OF HIGH FUNCTIONING

This period of time in our lives, especially for Marilynn, encompassed very high functioning and then a first, gradual, but palpable descent into her mental regression. At first, it was mildly mental, growing more so slowly over time, and requiring more complicated compromises (the "enabling" referred to earlier). It did not yet require distinct changes in my routines and responses, but they were to come, closer to the "end."

Marilynn had completed her Master's Degree in marriage and family counseling. She had also completed her field-work hours that would count toward eventual licensing as a Marriage and Family Therapist (MFT). As she was getting ready to begin her internship hours, leading toward licensing, our lives took a turn. She was anxious about the eventual exam she would have to take when she finished her intern hours. But she was willing to plow ahead.

At the same time, my involvement with the Feuerstein Institute in Jerusalem was intensifying. I was spending increasing amounts of time there, especially as I entered an "early retirement" phase in my university career. Marilynn loved being in Israel with me, the friends we made, and the activities we were engaged in while there. But there were times when she did not want to travel, as she had begun to work with children and adults with a "learning disabilities" as a cognitive therapist, applying what she was learning from our Feuerstein activities. By this time we both had had more than 10 years of exposure. For her, it was the consequence of participating in many training seminars and both observing and providing help to children using the methods.

Then an unexpected development occurred. In our many previous times in the country we stayed in hotels, in borrowed apartments, and for a 6-month stay rented our own apartment. Then in 2001, we rented a small apartment in the center of Jerusalem, in a lovely somewhat upscale neighborhood (nearby the President's residence). Up to that time, she had adamantly refused to consider buying our own place. "The Institute is too crazy a place to work in and I don't want to own another residence" she would say. But events conspired, and with my retirement from the university, the prospects of our spending more time in Israel loomed. Also the growing involvement she experienced in the Institute, and the lovely neighborhood we were living in changed her mind. She surprised me by saying "perhaps we should look for a place of our own," and feel settled into our new life?

And so we did, a few months later we found a lovely apartment in a beautiful part of Jerusalem, somewhat away from the center and all of its noise and busy pace. We made our decision rapidly… we saw it at 10 AM, made a bid at 12 noon, and it was accepted at 3 PM. We moved in two days later, as we acquired it with all its furnishing, including a full kitchen, and much of the previous owner's clothing (that her children later came to claim). We felt at home in our adopted country, and again experienced the pleasure of building our "nest."

Those early years were joyous. We would leave the apartment early each morning, on our way to the Institute, and stand for a moment at the top of the outer stairs of the building, and say to one another "I wonder what adventure awaits us today!" And there were adventures, be they in Jerusalem where we worked, or somewhere in the world where our work took us.

Initially, Marilynn wanted to accumulate hours toward her eventual marriage and family therapist license, and we were able to make arrangements in the Institute for a social worker to supervise her. But at the same time she began to sit in on every training seminar in the Institute, learning the assessment techniques, the programs to teach cognitive functioning, and how to mediate them to learning disabled individuals. She also sat in on every seminar that I gave abroad, and there were many as we traveled to many counties in Europe, Africa, South America, and back in the US. She loved the travel, was engaged in the seminar learning, eventually started to coach seminar participants and offer instructional interventions.

The transition made sense logistically, as we were so intensively involved in Israel and the Institute's activities, and it connected with her previous experiences as a teacher.

When she traveled with me abroad to do training seminars, she never wanted to "teach an instrument or procedure" but had meaningful insights to share during discussions, and she shared them with participants practicing the techniques they were learning.

She had brought much of this into her functional repertoire before we started to live in Jerusalem. It was greatly intensified as we lived in the country for greater and greater periods of time. She eventually gave up her intention to seek the marriage and family license in California and focused on the mediated learning experience approach that is the basis of the "Feuerstein" applications that we were immersed in. As I think about this transition for her I see it from two perspectives: the deeply engaging, both personally and professionally, aspects of the mediated learning formats embedded in the Feuerstein programs and applications, as she acquired the skills involved, and perhaps to a lesser degree her anxiety related to the process of completion of her marriage and family requirements.

The consequence of this, particularly after our deeper engagement in the Institute's work, was that she became an excellent mediator, assessing learning development needs in clients, and in mediational teaching to help overcome cognitive functioning deficits. There was a continuity, as in the mediated learning approach a great deal of counseling process is involved, reflecting a continuity that was a major part of her MA degree program.

A second consequence was that Professor Feuerstein, our mentor, saw her skills, had confidence in her and began giving her difficult clients to work with. Sometimes she was part of a team of mediators and often worked alone. During this period I recall observing her work and watching her develop into a very sensitive, creative, and effective professional. This was also amplified by her involvement in our many training and consulting experiences abroad.

There were several instances when we were abroad, especially when we were in a place for an extended period of time, Marilynn would work with difficult cases, and together we would apply the mediated learning strategies of the Feuerstein approach. It was a time of collaboration, as both of us deepened our knowledge and skills.

There was another important aspect to our travels abroad. There is something in the mediated learning approach, aside from its great success in helping to overcome cognitive and behavioral deficits, many of which are quite severe. As the process is applied, we bring the significant others in the client's life—parents, spouses, teachers, siblings, etc.—into significant interactions. They observe, we consult, we engage in problem-solving. Meaningful relationships are formed, and in those instances when we would return to a venue, as we often did, even if working with other clients and families, we would find ourselves renewing and intensifying these relationships. I came to see this dynamic in this way and have conveyed this to others: the nature of the mediational interaction is that once we enter the lives of the child or family we are there forever. A bit romantic perhaps, but repeatedly experienced.

Testament to this occurred much later. After Marilynn's regression that ultimately prevented her from traveling with me, and following her death, when I was abroad and people inquired about Marilynn and I told them about her state and demise, there were almost always tears in the eyes of those who knew her. She was much loved!

PROCESSING WHAT WAS TO COME

Before continuing to recount the details of these years, and her gradual descent into her personal oblivion, I think about my personal sense of my denial and how that contributed to the nature of our relationship as it progressed into Marilynn's decline into dementia. I have come to know (and accept) that I am very intellectually defended, so at the time I did not react emotionally to the implications of her regression but instead placed it into an intellectual context. It was my "understanding it," analyzing the changes of behavior, and making acceptable (for me) accommodations. I didn't get angry—at least at the time I didn't (could not?) acknowledge it. I don't even recall feeling much frustration. My inner feeling was "let's get on with it" and make things work. By making things work I needed to make Marilynn comfortable, and restore equilibrium, for both of us. I now see that I was continuously reframing our changed interaction so as not to feel loss—until the very end when the interaction was so changed that it infiltrated my sense of my caretaking role.

I have subsequently learned that this was probably my particular way of dealing with the situations that Marilynn confronted me (and our relationship) with. How different it might have been from that which many intimate partners who become caregivers experience I cannot know. But for me, I contented myself with the feeling of successful resolution of the problematic situations that were encountered. The adjustments worked, early on, and we could get on with our interesting life. And my feeling of love did not diminish.

But back to denial and enabling. For us, and me, denial was the mechanism for my enabling. It led to positive adjustments to routines and responses, and sustained both involvement and Marilynn's sense of being in the world. She did not know or accept when confronted, that she was regressing. The details that follow illustrate this reframing. It was only at the very end, when Marilynn was truly and fully gone and had been so for several years that I began to get in touch with my denial, and the depression that accompanied the salient experience of loss. And with this, I had the help of a new and emotionally liberating relationship with a newly acquired loving partner, Vera. This is an important part of the story that deserves its chapter of telling.

PRECIPITANT AND PROXIMAL EVENTS

During these years I was asked to travel a great deal. Much of our work in the Feuerstein Institute involved training and consulting with people all over the world, disseminating the programs that people wanted to learn and apply. Marilynn loved travelling, and was familiar and expert in the applications. So for many of these trips, she accompanied me. While still in San Francisco, I've described how she had a small clientele of children and adults with whom she was using the Feuerstein approach. In those times she did not want to interrupt the therapy, and so stayed at home when I travelled to Israel and other places abroad. One signal that things were deteriorating occurred in the middle of one of my trips to South Africa in the early 2000's before Marilynn was showing manifest symptoms. I was away for three weeks.

Here I must make an important diversion before continuing to recount the incident above. For a number of years our son David had labeled me "the great communicator." This was a term of derision, as I would for long periods of time not telephone or not make contact in other ways. When living in apartments within 50 feet of one another in San Francisco, or during our extended times in Israel, we would go for weeks and weeks not speaking or writing to one another. Leaving aside the dynamics of such behavior, this may have been a precipitant in Marilynn's decline that my lack of communicational inclinations caused. In a telephone call to my son I learned that Marilynn was upset because she did not know where I was, what I was doing, when I would return, and was anxious and confused, in spite of several phone calls I had with her. She was disoriented about shopping for groceries (she was still driving at this time), and David was concerned about her ability to be alone. And this was at a relatively early stage in her descent! In retrospect, if I had called her with some frequency during that trip, told her of my activities, asked her to describe her situation at home, I might have prevented her reaction and confusion.

During the whole period described here, from the beginning well into the need to take her from Israel back to the US and place her in a residential care facility, we would go to Professor Feuerstein's home almost every evening, where he and I would work on projects and Marilynn would sit at the side of the room listening and occasionally introjecting a question or comment about what he and I were discussing. Usually her comments were on point, occasionally not. When I got annoyed with the interruption and would react, Professor Feuerstein would signal me that I was being unnecessarily impatient (usually by looking at me sternly over his glasses, with a disapproving facial expression, sometimes waving a finger). Even toward the very end of our time in Israel, Marilynn would come and sit with us. Interestingly, on the drive back to our home was the only time Marilynn would initiate conversations, usually reflecting on some concept or process that the Professor and I had been working on. I saw that as an accessing of deeply held knowledge that brought her back to cogency, overcoming much of the neurological deficiency that she was experiencing.

Back to our travelling experiences bringing Feuerstein to the world. During the training seminars Marilynn would never teach directly but would sit with participants when they were working in small groups or practicing techniques. She would observe, offer suggestions, and was valued as a "coach." Two incidents come to mind from this time.

We were in Mumbai, India. I was conducting a seminar on one of the Feuerstein techniques to a group of about 25 participants. Marilynn was sitting with the group, quietly and not interacting. Our host came into the room and whispered to her that a sightseeing trip around the city was being arranged for her. She whispered back “I cannot go, I am needed here!” In one of the last such experiences that Marilynn could participate in, I had to leave the room for approximately an hour, and I gave the participants an independent activity to complete. I did not learn until several years later that when I left the room Marilynn got up, went to the whiteboard, and started to teach one of the instruments of the program.

This is after at least 20 years of her never wanting to take such a role. When I asked what precipitated this response from her, the speculation was that while she was sitting with one of the small groups working on a project, some confusion was expressed, and she went to the board “to explain it.” At the time I did not know it happened, would have been totally surprised, and in retrospect wonder if she could have recounted the experience to me had I asked her about it.

On another one of our trips, this time to Dallas, Texas, when Marilynn’s symptoms were more palpable but not overtly interfering with her functioning, after the first three days of the seminar Marilynn complained of severe pain in her lower abdomen. She was in great pain. When I took her to a hospital emergency room it was determined that she had a blood clot in her upper thigh, and that she needed immediate hospitalization. Although I felt that she was mentally aware of her circumstances, the attending hospital staff also identified some confusion in her response. She was hospitalized for 6 days, and then transferred back to California for further treatment. The training seminar was postponed, and I stayed with her in Dallas and then San Francisco.

One aspect of this event was that she was placed on an anti-clotting mediation that required periodic blood testing and for the first several weeks’ injections three times a day. I have a strong aversion (phobic reaction) to injections, for myself and even when observing others. So much so that earlier in our marriage, and she needed injections for allergies, I could not give them to her. In this instance, requiring three injections each day, as a serious medical matter, I forced myself to do it, almost passing out each time I had to inject her. Fortunately, my duress seemed not to bother her at all, and after a few weeks, she was placed on another medication that did not require the injections, or taking her several times a week for blood tests. She did not seem to be particularly aware of this whole process and was a passive participant throughout.

As Marilynn's dementia deepened, her love of travel combined with my inability to leave her alone in Jerusalem caused me to continue to have her accompany me on the international trips. I had two options—arrange a caregiver in the place we were going, which was often quite possible, or take a care giving person with us. I had not yet made the "at home" arrangements that occurred later. Here enters Judy Delphia. Judy is a registered nurse and a specialist in the training of home health care practitioners, so she brought both expertise and a deeply caring relationship into the picture. Fifteen years earlier she had taken care of my mother, in extraordinary ways, until her passing. And through this had forged a deep personal relationship with Marilynn and me. She had been following the course of events with Marilynn from afar, living in Kansas City. I began to call Judy, in the US, and propose an adventure for her. "How would you like to meet us in Paris (or India, Holland, Taiwan, etc.), or come to Israel, and be with Marilynn while I did the things required of me?" She always said yes, and so began several years of mutually shared caregiving adventures. During the time Judy took care of my mother, she had participated with us in providing cognitive stimulation for her (the "Feuerstein" techniques) and so was familiar with the approach, even taking some training seminars on her own, and spending time in Jerusalem working at the Institute. Sitting in with Marilynn at the various seminars and events that were part of the international trips enhanced her knowledge (that she later put to use in planning with the Institute cognitive modifiability interventions for the elderly population that was her professional specialty).

In these various situations, on the trips where I was training and consulting, Judy would sit with Marilynn in the seminars, taking her away when she was restless, bringing her back for some of the social interactions, all in a smooth and seamless way, so that Marilynn felt (and was) a part of things. We would have our meals together, socialize with others in the group, go for walks in the downtime. I particularly recall our joining a group to walk along the Seine in Paris, going from the University of Paris campus all the way to Notre Dame, stopping to see gardens, a small zoo, with Marilynn and Judy and I and a larger group of about 10 people enjoying the experience. Another time, again in Paris, going to a shopping district with a friend who knew how to navigate the subways. As Marilynn's abilities declined, to tolerate the physical activity, process the scene around her, and focus, Judy would adjust the expectations and assess Marilynn's needs and abilities. Thus Marilynn sustained travel and maintained an involvement in spite of her growing debilitation. Again, perhaps this was another experience that slowed down the progression of her deterioration.

I was increasingly aware that Marilynn's gradual descent encompassed several phases, sometimes overlapping but generally distinct and progressive. This has become much clearer to me in retrospect as I write this. There were several. She went through a wandering phase that I internally labeled her "fugue" state. I viewed it as reflecting a sense of confusion and anxiety. It was followed by a phase of incontinence, where she lost the ability to anticipate her physical needs and would soil or wet herself without awareness that it was occurring. Then there was a period of delusional behavior, where her inability to distinguish reality from fantasy, or inner promptings, caused her to be increasingly anxious. In this phrase, I had to monitor what we watched on television, or respond to an action or emotion that came from this inability to distinguish and understand what she was observing or experiencing. Lastly, toward the end, but still able to convey her feelings, a phase of withdrawal. Here she did not want to get out of bed, did not want to go to her daycare setting, which she had loved, and would get angry and abusive of me when I forced her to get up, get dressed, and move out into her day (I will describe more of this in the next chapter). What were the phases like, and how did I deal with them?

In the fugue state, the concern she had was related to her confusion regarding where she was and where I was, if not directly physically present, and the anxiety that she experienced. If alone, whether in our apartment or my office where she sat and read while I worked, she would leave and search for me. If I went out to do a task or talk to someone, when I returned she would be gone. Sometimes wandering about the 4 floors of the building we worked in, sometimes out of the building into the immediate neighborhood. Usually, I could find her, often with the help of those who knew her and could guide me on her route. I would guide her back, gently explaining and reassuring her.

During this phrase, I could not leave her alone in the apartment. Our neighbors would find her wandering through the five-floor building

and calling out for me. While together in the apartment I would engage the deadbolt lock to keep her inside. Early on in this phrase she was able to tell me that she was looking for me. In later stages in the phrase she would just look at me blankly, wondering about my concern. On more than one occasion when left alone in the apartment she would engage the deadbolt lock, then fall asleep, not responding to my ringing the bell, knocking on the door, or calling her on the telephone. Fortunately, I could go to the next-door apartment, and climb from their balcony to ours, from the outside. It was five floors up, and frightened our neighbors. Ultimately, after that encounter, I removed the deadbolt. But that meant that when in the apartment with her I had to be very alert to her movements, particularly when we were in different rooms. More than once I heard her leave and had to retrieve her.

More troublesome incidents occurred when she was asked to stay put when I left her in the car to go into a grocery store (and she assured me that she would not leave) while sitting in my office and she got out into the neighborhood adjacent to the office building, or leave the apartment unnoticed. When asked, in those occasions when she could respond (which became increasingly difficult for her) she would say "I was looking for you." But there were times when we had to search an unfamiliar neighborhood or figure out where she might go in an airport waiting for area.

Some examples: While we were waiting to board a flight and sitting at a table in the general boarding area, I asked if she would stay at the table while I got a magazine for us. She said yes, and I reinforced the importance of her not leaving, and checked for her understanding. When I returned a few minutes later she was gone. I went to the information booth, explained the situation, and was escorted in an electric vehicle around the various concourses of the airport to try to find her. At first, it seemed like a futile search until we spotted an attendant walking her out of one of the concourses, taking her I presume to the emergency facilities. What had happened? She was found lined up at a departure gate to get on a flight, for which she had no passport or tickets. I vowed that I would not make that mistake again!

Another such instance from her fugue state was when we were in the car together, and wanted to buy something from a grocery store not in our immediate neighborhood. This was in Israel where neither one of us spoke the language and were not familiar with the particular surroundings of the neighborhood where the store was. I said to her "Marilynn, I am going into the store to buy just a few things (juice, milk, some fruit). It will be a short time. You can come in with me or stay in the car." She responded "I will stay in the car." I would repeat how important it was for her not to leave the car. She assured me that she would not. When I returned she was gone! What to do? First I called my dearest Israeli friend Ami Shitrit for help. He immediately suggested that he come to where we were and look for her. I suggested a less intrusive response since he was on the other side of the city and working. He suggested calling the Israeli equivalent of "911." So I did that. In the meantime, the clerks in the Arab market where this incident took place went out to search the immediate surroundings, with no luck. Then the police came in response to the emergency call, searched a wider scope of the neighborhood, and found her sitting in a small park in the center of the Arab neighborhood adjacent to the market. When she was found she had no memory of the preceding events and no emotional response (neither fear nor surprise). Needless to say, I never left her in the car alone again, anywhere or no matter the time duration of the separation.

In these instances, perhaps she was looking for me, not remembering that I had said that I would return. I knew that I would never know, so did not press the issue. My response was to make internal mental adjustments, saying to myself: "I must remember not to leave her alone. Getting her verbal assent is not meaningful. It is not her fault. She must be protected." And perhaps most importantly, for me: "I can find ways to make this situation comfortable for both Marilynn and myself." Until the very end, I did! I do not recall feelings of anger at moments like this. Perhaps the label "fugue" is not accurate. She was not "running away from something" but rather simply forgetting where I was, where she was, and her assurances that she would stay put! For Marilynn, this fugue state lasted only a few months, fortunately for both of us. Others preceded or followed, I presume related to the gradual cortical deterioration that was occurring and fragments of her awareness and confusing aspects of the social situations she found herself not understanding or knowing how to cope.

I cannot recall whether her incontinence phase preceded, overlapped, or followed the fugue phase. In approximately 2011, five years before she devolved into almost full regression, she began to lose the ability to signal (to herself) or be aware of her toileting needs. I, and others, would see her staining her clothing, smell her, and I would have to get her to a toilet and clean her up. She had little awareness of her condition. We made the transition to disposable undergarments. She did not resist, I don't think she understood the difference. My evidence for this conclusion was that when travelling, her habit had been to wash her underpants each night so they would be fresh for the morning. It took me many months to convince her that what she was wearing was disposable. When she got it, she had a hard time distinguishing her undergarments from the outer, and more than once she tried to discard what she was wearing. In those instances I retrieved things from the trash in airports and restaurants. Then (in another needed accommodation) we always used the family restrooms in airports or other facilities so I could help her with the processes involved.

When out in the world, it was necessary to try to anticipate her needs. Sometimes successfully and sometimes not. In this phase her lack of awareness and concern was something of a blessing, as there was no embarrassment or anxiety, on her part.

As this phrase settled into routine our functioning simply took the form of periodic taking her to a restroom, checking on her state, and encouraging her to function.

Her delusional phase could be termed "passive." By that, I mean that she was reactive (to stimuli) rather than initiatory. If she saw a film that was "scary" she would want to turn off all the lights, close and lock the doors, so "that the monsters would not come in and attack us." Once when watching an emotional film about a mother who would not accept the love of her child, Marilynn began to talk about her being a mother, of having children, worried if she had loved them enough, would they love her, all with a kind of anxious, repetitive, "driven" quality that took an hour or so to dissipate. This went on for many hours after the film had ended. When I attempted to engage her in a discussion about the film and her reactions, she did not respond to me, but simply repeated her concerns, several times. After seeing a film about a tragedy in outer space she did not want to leave her seat in the cinema after the film concluded.

When I went to the neurologists who were treating her and asked for some medication to deal with the delusional thinking they were not cooperative. I felt that a mild anti-psychotic might help they did not agree, saying in effect that "she has a deteriorative condition, and we should just let it run its course." I did not accept this, and when I consulted with her primary care physician, who fortunately agreed with me and prescribed medication. It helped, and her delusional thinking almost completely subsided.

A complication of traveling in airports, at the time when she could not walk any distances, was that she was frightened of riding in the transport carts provided. She felt that they were going too fast and she wanted to get off. She would reach for the walls and support rails as the vehicle moved, greatly endangering herself and the other passengers. No amount of verbal assurance mollified her, and we had to abandon that mode of transport. Even wheelchairs were difficult, especially if the person pushing them went too fast. In this instance, I resorted to finding an unoccupied chair and pushing it myself (against the rules in many airports). So if we had the time when transferring or going in or out we walked slowly, sat down a lot, and got where we needed to be, albeit slowly. And we did miss a few flights!

Another aspect of her confused mental state had some risks for me! When her physical equilibrium became uncertain, several potentially difficult situations arose. Once in a shopping center parking lot as

I was walking next to her, but not holding her arm, she tripped over a curb and fell. As I bent over to pick her up she starts screaming that I had pushed her. Just at that moment, a police car pulled up, the officer got out, thinking that he had come upon a domestic abuse situation. It took considerable explaining, but he was understanding and accepting. After that incident I made sure to hold her hand and monitor her movements more carefully.

However, while holding on to her on a very congested downtown Melbourne, Australia street, while waiting to board a streetcar, she fell and pulled me down on top of her. Then started yelling loudly "You pushed me down, you pushed me down!" Fortunately, the rushing crowd of people did not pay any attention to us, and I got her up, and into the streetcar. Needless to say, both of these incidents heightened my vigilance regarding her physical responses to movement. It was clear that her future in this regard was getting close to the limits.

INDICATIONS OF SERIOUS DECLINE

How to characterize the changes, conveying the seriousness and significance of Marilynn's decline? I saw it in her withdrawal. Many of the details of this will come in the next chapter. Like the rest of the story, the end was signaled not so much in what she initiated or could communicate, as she began to lose her ability to introspect, but in her responses to the various accommodations that I made. She was loving, accepting, and seemed to implicitly accept the growing limitations on her activities…unless she was confronted, and then she would deny. "You are making me more disabled than I am!" was a frequent response. But it was becoming clear to me that we were moving into another and perhaps climactic phase in our lives together.

6

Coming to the End:

Mourning the Loss

Jerusalem-San Francisco
2016-2019

The title of this chapter indicates my awareness at the time that our lives as I had known and loved them were coming to an end. For Marilynn and myself. Changes had to be contemplated and made. I had to acknowledge and act. My recollection of that time was that it was a continuation of what had preceded…a "get on with it." As always, I was thoughtful and contemplative, not necessarily the most healthy place to be. It was only much later that I slowly recognized that I might have been depressed. But that is part of the story to come.

At this point, I must acknowledge a major debt I owe to Barry Peterson, the author of Jan's Story (2010) so much so that I included him in the dedications. His book is the personal story of his relationship with his wife Jan and the experience of being with her as she declined into early-onset Alzheimer's. Throughout that deeply moving book he refers to her condition as "the Disease," and recounts the ways in which she slowly lost her memory, and its effects on their deeply loving relationship, leading to the need to place her in residential care and his journey toward seeking a new life for himself.

The book was given to me by a friend, amid my growing loneliness and yet unacknowledged depression. By that time I had placed Marilynn in a residential care facility in the San Francisco Bay Area, and returned to Israel alone to continue my professional life. The book is less than 200 pages. I read it in the evenings, sitting alone in the apartment in Jerusalem that Marilynn and I had furnished, and loved during our almost 15 years in residence there. It took me several weeks to read the first 20 very brief chapters describing Barry and Jan's meeting and life together. Then came the final chapters describing Barry's encouragement from friends to seek a new life for himself, translated into finding a woman whom he could love, and recapture that essential part of himself. I read this part of the book in one evening, with tears streaming down, finally feeling a connection and access into what I now knew I must have been repressing for several years. It also told me what I must do to get on with my life, without guilt or remorse. It was the right thing to do! I write the previous sentence because I want the reader to understand and take comfort from the vicissitudes of difference one experiences in this journey. His was the experience of a rapid onset as many such disease courses are. Mine was gradual, over years, and even in the final stages that eventually took 5 years, went slowly and inexorably. But I express my gratitude to Barry for his book that helped me to acknowledge what I was feeling deep down but not recognize and deal with. Thus the details of my experience are in some ways similar to Barry's but also with many differences. They follow in this chapter.

Linking Barry's experience and mine leads me to observe that the course of dementia has many permutations. Did Marilynn have Alzheimer's disease? I have not used this term thus far in this narrative. That is because, and especially with my background, I am skeptical of the diagnosis, generally and for Marilynn in particular. With her long course of regression, the very mixed signals, and— for me—the relative imprecision of the diagnostic tests, it may or may not have been. And I must confess, being her long time lover, husband, companion, and ultimately her caregiver, it did not matter much to me "what" she had. It was more important to meet her needs, and mine, in a comfortable and workable environment. And that happened. Much of this is portrayed in the previous chapter.

SIGNS INTO SIGNALS

As I see it signs are indications, sometimes vague, always inconsistent, that create awareness. Signals are more discrete cues that presage actions. The first signs were in 2010, at the time of our 50th wedding anniversary. I had arranged that our immediate family— David and his marital partner Todd, Alan and his wife Loraine and our three grand daughters Elizabeth, Rosemary, and Sarah— meet us in Barcelona for a celebratory cruise of the Mediterranean. While Marilynn was able to do all of the physical things—the shore excursions, the social interactions, and enjoy being with her family— it was clear that she did not fully understand the reasons for the celebration. Then in 2011, the signs turned into signals. She became incontinent, she began losing track of where she was, and the fugue states became increasingly frequent. It was these changes in her level of functioning, much of which has been described in the previous chapter that led to actions that needed to be taken.

One action was to take her to a neurologist, who assessed her and confirmed her dysfunctions, but could not establish a definitive diagnosis. It might be early Parkinson's, or perhaps Alzheimer's. ALS was not mentioned. He did not prescribe any tests such as CT Scans or MRI, but this was in Israel, we were seeing him as a private practitioner, but it planted a seed. When back in the US I took her to our medical care provider, they conducted CT Scan, and told me that they thought she had lost 25% of her brain capacity. I know I am being vague here, but it was a long time ago, and given my proclivities described above, I don't have specific recall of the details.

COLLATERAL EVENTS

Another event intruded on our life, with implications for the issue of diagnosis and labeling. After Marilynn had been placed into the residential care environment for approximately a year, and as she was moving more overtly into her dementia, our older son Alan contracted and eventually died of a rare variant of ALS. It's name is Frontal Temporal Lateral Dementia (FTLD). Around the time of his diagnosis and rapid deterioration (8 months from the formal diagnosis to his death), a major genetic study was underway at the University of California, San Francisco. We (the family) were enrolled in the study. Sibling David was extensively studied—physically through blood studies, various non-invasive methods (CAT-Scan, MRI, and others that do not come to mind as I write), psychological assessments, and historical reconstructions. David went through the whole protocol. Marilynn participated in the early stages, but by the time they were ready to administer the non-invasive methodology (CAT-Scan, MRI, Spinal Tap, etc.) she was too regressed to participate. Upon Alan's passing, and Marilynn's passing, autopsies were conducted and their brains and spinal cords were analyzed by the research team.

The general direction of the research was the exploration of the genetic factors in producing the disease. They have determined that this form of ALS is genetically determined through mutations that are passed down from one generation to another, and may or may not manifest in symptoms (we were told generally according to a 10% incidence rate). Again, I know I am being very general here, and I hope you will excuse me. My goal here is to simply establish a platform for considering the nature of Marilynn's descent into her dementia, with Alzheimer's or some other mentally deteriorative condition being the cause. Along the way, after Alan's death but before Marilynn's, David got a "clean bill of health." He did not have the mutation. Other members of the family—sister, grandchildren— will need to decide and carry out genetic testing on their own.

Following Alan and Marilynn's passing, the research team analyzed the data from our family and concluded that there was a possibility that Marilynn shared some of the FTLD conditions, but within a narrow range of probability. There wasn't enough data to pin it down more precisely. With Marilynn's condition, I felt some degree of blessing, as she was always gentle and accepting, up until the very end of my caregiving ability, notwithstanding her denial of her condition, and my state of denial. I know many individuals with similar diagnostic profiles are angry, defiant, and difficult to care for. There are several such individuals within my network of familiarity who are like this. Marilynn was not. Even when she became defiant with me, after being placed i residential care she was always accepting and pliable with her caregivers.

Through the various stages of her mental deterioration, before they move into residential care, she had allowed me to take care of her. At first, the actions were subtle and mundane, akin to opening a door for her to pass through. If they were not specifically identified as to help for her diminishing functioning she accepted the accommodations. But not always.

In the early stages, still in San Francisco, I eventually realized that she should not be driving a car independently, initially because of her lack of memory for familiar places, like the supermarket or post office, For I envisioned her driving off into the sunset never knowing where she was supposed to be...or not be. The routes she was taking should have been familiar to her as she knew the neighborhood. And yet she would seemingly disappear, for hours at a time. When she did reappear, it was hard for her to tell us (myself, my son who lived nearby, and who had mobilized with me to call the highway patrol or the city police department) what had happened. As near as we could tell, she would take a wrong turn, and drive for hours before recognizing that she was not where she needed to be. How she eventually got home we never could ascertain. We never actually had to have the police find her, but endured hours of anxiety and concern. And when she did return she did not express anxiety, and she could not understand why we were worried. It was like her saying "what are you so concerned about, I am not bothered." It was that lack of empathy that began to be a cue for me as to what was happening. She was angry with me and protested that "I was making her more disabled than she was!" I equivocated. However, the final decision to terminate her driving occurred when I needed to have a medical procedure in a facility several hundred miles from San Francisco, and was told that I should not try to drive myself home. Marilynn said that she would come with me and drive me home. When David heard this he became adamant, insisted that she should not be driving, and declared that he would drive up to the facility and drive me home. It was at that point that my vacillation ended and we (David and I) took her keys away. She did not understand or accept it, and for many years later continued to be angry with me about the decision. Our children and friends felt relieved, telling me that for years they worried about her driving, especially when they were passengers in the car she was piloting. Several years later, whenever the subject came up she would tell me "I can drive, you just stopped me." When challenged further she would say "If I am alone in the car, and not distracted by someone else in the car, I can do it!

CAREGIVING IN THE THROES OF DEEPENING DECLINE

As Marilynn sank further into her dementia, she allowed me to intervene more actively in meeting her needs. In slightly later times back in Israel she would let me dress her, at first choosing what she wanted to wear, later accepting what I picked out for her. At first, selecting colors and matching outfits was important for her. She let me assist her with the toilet routines, washing her face, and brushing her teeth. We even laughed about some of the dementia-related aspects of this routine.

She began to repetitively verbalize the same phrase, "I've got to be up." It was perseverative and persists as long as she is awake, even in the short moments at night when she awakes, before she falls asleep again. The energy with which the verbalization waxes and wanes, and is reflected in the ways she says it, speed, amplitude, and phrasing (often devolving to "I gotta be…"). I have noticed that in public groups she is louder, and when others are talking she seems more insistent, but with the same words. She also seemed to be able to listen to conversations while verbalizing, occasionally interrupting herself to repeat a word she has heard in the conversation, or comment on some aspect of it that is meaningful to her. She can also be influenced to talk more softly, to recognize that others are having difficulty hearing what is going on, or need to focus on what others are saying.

The response does not last long, but she can calibrate the behavior upon my request. People often considered me a hero for the caregiving I gave Marilynn. didn't feel like a hero. Anything but…! I like to consider myself a person of commitments—I stay with and am loyal to those and that to which I engage, sometimes without considering the inner feelings, just a kind of "doing." With Marilynn at this stage, I began to see myself differently. I was not gentle, I was starting to lose patience with small events—getting her undressed, her eating all the crumbs off the dining table, disappearing into bedrooms to get into bed with her clothes still on, and a multitude of similar events simply indicating her lack of awareness of time, space, events—and I found myself yelling at her, moving her physically with some harshness, I certainly did not feel the hero. And later I chided myself for the loss of control. I didn't like myself at these moments. I had to remind myself that she did not know who and where she is. I recalled, and knew her essential gentleness. It hurt to see her blank face and unseeing eyes.

As dementia deepened, and I must force her out of bed, and she says "I hate you," she sometimes adds "right now," suggesting some sense of time and place? In these times of resistance, she says "I'll bite you! I'll step all over you! I'll hit you in your gonads (I always wondered where and how that word came into her vocabulary)!" And when she wants to get back into the bed, which became every morning, and I non-verbally blocked her way as I started to dress her, she would continually repeat the threats. It is so hard when the person you love and have taken care of tells you repeatedly that she hates you. When we go down the elevator to meet the van that will take her to her day activity program I would look into her eyes and make facial contact, and ask: "This morning, do you want to give me a kiss or bite me?" Her response varied, depending on how long her anger—that is real discomfort—lasts. I know it is not real anger, and that it will not be sustained, but it still hurts. I am learning the distinction between what is understood in one's head and felt in one's gut. Sometimes when she says "I'll bite you" I will put my arm in front of her face and she will smile at me—I have called her bluff. Once in a while, she will try to bite, and I will pull my hand away rapidly. By the time she boards the van most of the immediate past is gone, and later in the day when I see her after her activity group it is all forgotten, and the next day repeats itself in the same way.

As I said, getting up in the morning became increasingly difficult for her, and for me as the agent of her arising. She sleeps very soundly, a blessing, and can sleep for long hours—through 15 or 20 hours, being aroused only to use the toilet and then wanting to return to bed. On days where she has her activity group, that she went willingly to once up and dressed, at 8:15 or so I must wake her up. She resists and often must be forced to awake and get out of bed. In this condition, I must pull her covers off, with protestations of "I'm cold," even when the room is quite warm. I often must turn her legs toward the edge of the bed and pull her to a sitting position. Then she gets angry with all the threats described above. As we walk to the bathroom and she uses the toilet, the angry verbalisms continue (it is the only semi-spontaneous verbal interaction she has with me) through the teeth brushing, face washing, and hair brushing—all of which she lets me do, acting physically compliant while continuing the verbal hostility. After a while, usually no more than 10 minutes, she "summarizes" her state with "I am very angry with you, etc." But most interestingly, the "I hate you" and "I'm angry with you" are often followed by "…for the moment."

We leave the apartment, go down the elevator and outer stairs, and she gets into the van that comes to take her to her program. Often she has shifted her mood, may tell the caregiver on the van that she is "mad at me," but with anger dissipated, and kind of a laughing and ironic conveyance. And when I see her next, usually at 5:00 PM, after her day at the program and a few hours with her in-home caregiver, she greets me with a smile, a hug, and kiss (if I initiate it), and the events of the morning are forgotten (by her, but not necessarily by me, although I am getting better about it).

In one phase she was constantly voicing "I got to be up" which became an inarticulate mumbling. It did not stop during the teeth brushing, and which I labeled "gaga gugu time" for that is what it sounded like. For a long time, I would initiate the toileting routine saying "Are you ready for gaga gugu time?" and she would respond with a smile and twinkle in her eye.

I recall one incident fairly late in the progression of decline. It was Shabbat for us, still living in Israel. We had no invitations for either Friday evening dinner or the Saturday mid-day meal. These events are usually good breaks in a sedentary routine, for both of us—to be with friends, to have some activity, and to signal the end of the usual routine of the week. But this weekend we had no such activity scheduled. All Marilynn wanted to do was sleep. I got her up for the toilet breaks, and to eat something, but she was happy to return to the bed, and I did not interrupt this need. On Saturday, around mid-day she was ready to get up, and so after the toileting, I got her into the shower. This is something that she hates and resists mightily. In winter I only force it once a week, on Saturdays. In summer I try a mid-week shower—no hair washing, which she hates more than the shower. She has become hypersensitive to touch, so the water on her body is an "ouch," as is combing and brushing her hair, even touching her shoulders to give her what she once adored—massaging her shoulders and upper back. So on the Shabbat I am describing, after the mid-day toileting I got her into the shower (with all protestations, which I counter by saying that "you either do it on your own or I will force you in," and she semi-complies. She got in, with encouragement/coercion, I washed her, including her hair, the resistance diminished ("I need to be out of here, please let me get out, etc.), and the routine was completed. Drying her body, drying her hair ("I can't stand this!"), getting underwear on was an ordeal for both of us. Following this most unpleasant experience she wanted to get back into bed. She slept for another few hours, and then was ready to get up and eat something.

Later in the day, she got up and we watched television together, increasingly difficult because of the constant "I gotta get up," as she is sitting and watching. Usually, she seems not to follow what is on the screen, but this time we watched the coverage of a funeral, with several eloquent eulogies, and from time to time she would repeat a phrase or a word, so something was registering, in spite of the perseverative verbalizing.

During that time she started to shift her attention from watching the news to two new sources of interest: On the Discovery Channel, she liked the program "How Things Are Made," and on the National Geographic Channel she focused on programs like finding gold in the wilderness, building tree houses, and the like. She maintained focus on these programs. Dramatic programs were beyond her ability to comprehend and focus.

As I returned her to bed, on that Shabbat (and on many other evenings) after another short meal, it occurred to me that this day, and others, did not have any "I hate you, I'm going to bite you," as we got ready for bed and did the toileting. On the Shabbat I am remembering, when I mentioned this to her she smiled, made eye contact, and seemed to have some understanding. The next morning, at the forced getting up at 8:15 AM, we returned to the typical daily routine!

During this time Marilynn's eating behavior changed in some interesting ways. At the beginning of the major decline, she would eat voraciously, everything on the plate, rapidly and in quantity. Then she began to slow down, and eat in a very distracted manner, chewing incessantly but not swallowing. (Much later I began to wonder whether the swallowing difficulty was related to possible ALS symptoms, being sensitized to them from our son Alan's diagnosis) Especially if she was tired she often needed help putting food on her fork, and bringing it to her mouth. Then she almost lost her ability to use a knife, and fork, eating everything with her hands. I used to joke that if the food required utensils, she would use her hands, and if the food was "finger food," like pizza, she would struggle to use a knife and fork. But in the period I am describing everything is picked up with the hand, even foods distinctly non-suited. And the other characteristic is taking a long time. She began sitting at the table for an hour (without intervention), slowly eating, self-distracting, mumbling ("I gotta be up" devolves into an "aggah, aggah," stopping only when her mouth is full), and needing to be reminded to swallow what is in her mouth.

COGNITIVE INTERVENTIONS

Marilynn's levels of functioning continued to deteriorate, but she was still able to spend the day with me at the Institute. The Institute had a clinic devoted to working with people who had various degrees of cognitive deficiency, and one of my activities was to consult and guide some of their activities. Marilynn was offered cognitive therapy. This was prior to involving her in the daycare program described below and lasted almost one year.

Her typical day during this period was to come with me to the Institute, sit in my office while I worked, usually reading and interacting with those who came to discuss various projects. She was known by everyone and would listen to our interactions and make relevant comments. Inserted into this day were four or five "therapy" sessions a week with a member of the clinic's therapy team. She enjoyed this, and the therapist enthusiastically told me that not only did she like working with Marilynn but that she was responding well and improving aspects of her mental processes. Marilynn was exposed to various activities from the Feuerstein Instrumental Enrichment (FIE) program, and variations based on it. The work-related to focusing, verbal responding, aspects of memory, perceptual discrimination, sustaining attention, and the like. Since Marilynn had been a teacher/therapist using FIE prior to her mental deterioration, aspects of the intervention were familiar to her. Her therapist related to me that from time to time Marilynn would recall some aspect of the program from her days of using it and they would talk about it.

Since this occurred during Marilynn's "fugue" phase, I would take her down to the clinic, on another floor of the building, and pick her up when the session was finished. This gave me a chance to get some feedback regarding what had happened. Often on the way back to my office, Marilynn would talk about what she was "learning" in the sessions.

As I think about this aspect of Marilynn's experience, I believe it slowed down the progression of her decline. I regretted that we could not continue this when she began the daycare program. However, perhaps it made her more alert and able to respond to the daycare activities she was exposed to, at least until her decline became more severe.

MARILYNN'S DAY CARE PROGRAM

As the situation became more demanding for me, and she could not be with me as I worked in the Institute, I consulted with a social worker who specialized in elderly clients. She guided me to an adult daycare program in Jerusalem, Melabev. I visited it and felt it would meet her needs. She was enrolled, and I met with the staff to describe her to them. The program was for English-speaking elderly with dementia. The participants sat 6 to a table. A small bus came to our apartment every day at 9:00 AM, took her to the program, and brought her back at around 3:00 PM. They had their meals together, including breakfast, and during the day would be encouraged to sing songs, listen to people talking about things relevant to their lives, and the like.

The first time I took Marilynn to Melabev, the daycare group setting for seniors with dementia, and watched her in the group, was the moment that I broke through my denial. Up to then a major part of my framing was that if she just tried harder, and paid attention to "what she knew, what she could do" things would be better. And I had begun to nag her, reminding her, chiding her for her lapses— "push the button to make the elevator come! Loosen the straps on your sandals to take them off! Use the fork to eat your food!!"—all with annoyance from me and a sense that she "could but would not" do the most simple of things. "Marilynn, the food that should be eaten with a fork you eat with your hands, and the food that is supposed to be eaten with your hands you try to use the fork!! And so on. But watching her on that first morning at Melebev I saw that she was in fact truly disabled, and that even more so, as demented or more so than many of the others, many of whom were considerably older. I walked out of that 10 minute observation with tears in my eyes, but also with a sense of "OK, I know what the situation is, I cannot, and should not, be pushing her to do what she obviously cannot, and that it is not a matter of her will, and not directed against me (even when she is angry with me for forcing her to do something she does not want, like getting out of bed in the morning).

So I began to understand her resistances, such as at times when she did not want to get out of bed in the morning that I described above. She was only articulate and fluent when she was angry. It was much less an emotionally hurtful thing for me, most of the time.

From time to time I interpreted and verbalized her reaction as "You don't hate me, you hate getting up in the morning and getting out of bed…" and she would acknowledge this, but it did not affect the repeated, perseverative verbalizing of "I hate you," even immediately responding "yes" to my reframing.

Again, at the end of my caretaking days, since she likes getting ready for bed, and getting into bed, the evening routines were just the opposite of the mornings—cooperative, open to some humor, and happy to do and complete her routines. We end it with "is it bedtime for Bonzo?" alluding to the famous Ronald Regan "B" movie that he starred in and that we joked about at bedtime from the earliest day of our marriage. And she sleeps soundly until the next day's repeat scenario.

WINDOWS OF COGENCY

Although Marilynn gradually became mentally and cognitively more limited, there were brief windows of cogency. At Melabev they have described how Marilynn will occasionally call over a caregiver to help someone at her table whom she sees needs assistance. In the early days of Melabev she would occasionally come home repeating the fragment of a song, or repeatedly saying something like "it is important to...save water, or respect people's rights." In more recent days, 6-8 months into her Melabev experience that does not happen. Her dementia is growing deeper.

For almost one year the program was wonderful for her, and me. She loved it and knew that it was a part of her day. I would wake her, toilet her, get her dressed, and take her down to the front of our apartment and she would get on the bus that would take her to the program. When she got on the bus I could see her "open up" and relate to the caregiver on the bus and the others who were going to the program. She came home with snatches of songs she had heard, or fragmentary details of cooking or foods that she had eaten and even telling me some details of a story that I assume had been read in the activity groups. She was responding to the content of the program.

So that I could continue my routines, I hired a wonderful young woman of Indian descent to meet her at the bus, bring her upstairs, change her clothes and clean her if she needed it, and make her comfortable, usually in front of the television. It was in this phase of her decline that she began to watch the Discovery channel, and especially programs that showed how commonly known things were made in factories—medicines, toys, books, etc. As I described, I would come in at

the end of my day, come over to the couch she was lying on, bend over and kiss her hello that she responded to.
Yet there were other cues that we were nearing the end of the phase of our relationship where I would be able to be her primary caregiver. One important indicator was related to the daycare program. Her resistance became more defiant, with the behaviors I described above. Every morning became a small fight as I described earlier, but with more intensity. After verbal encouragement, I had to physically move her into position to get dressed and into the bathroom. But when the fight was over and we were downstairs getting on the bus, the resistance subsided and she went willingly off to the program.

There were other signs. She could not walk more than a few steps without extreme fatigue. If she didn't have dinner before 6:00 in the evening she would not eat. "I need to go to bed!" She started resisting the toileting routines that had been well established and accepted by her. These and other things were clear indications that she needed to be in full-time care, and that I could not be her primary caregiver any longer. When the arrangements were made and we were leaving the country in a few days to take Marilynn to San Francisco and put her into a residential dementia care program I visited the program to thank them for the care they had given her. As I thanked them they said "We are going to miss Marilynn. When someone at her table needs help, she calls one of the caregivers over." This shocked me. There was still something there.

That was evidenced by a series of events a few years earlier. We were scheduled to do a training seminar in Hong Kong. It was for one week, in one physical location, and our hosts were well known to us from previous encounters. Marilynn came with me and with our hosts and the training venue (the seminar offered in the same hotel where we were staying) we did not need an attending caregiver. Three or four days before we were scheduled to leave we found out that Marilynn's brother had died. The original message was that he would be buried immediately and that the family would come together for a memorial a month or so later. So we went off to Hong Kong. While in Hong Kong we learned that the plans had changed, that the funeral would be delayed for two weeks following his death, and that the family would assemble in San Diego for it.

Marilynn had come from a large, engaged, and supportive extended family, and I asked her if she wanted to go. She did and so I made plans. We were to fly back to Israel, spend a few days there (with Professor Feuerstein), and then go to California for the funeral. Since we were traveling to California our plan was to spend a month or so in San Francisco, where we have an apartment and be with our family and friends. I made these plans, and as was increasingly becoming the case, I did not know to what extent Marilynn was registering or remembering all this. I frequently reminded her that her brother had died and that we were going back to be with the family for his funeral. During the four days we were in Israel, Professor Feuerstein was quite ill—he had a serious bronchial infection, was on heavy doses of antibiotics, and had difficulty breathing and talking. He was, as a 92 year old, quite weak. But he had to "work," and we sat with him for short periods of time talking about projects and things that were in his mind.

It was a Monday evening. We were due to leave for the US on Tuesday morning. When we went to him he was very tired, and it was difficult for him to talk. After about 45 minutes he said that he had to rest, that he would miss us, that he understood why we were going, and that "I hope God gives us two more years to finish our work," when we returned. We said goodbye, and that we would call him the next morning before we got on the airplane. When we called his son Aharon answered the phone and said that he was still sleeping, that they were having difficulty waking him up, but they would relate our greetings to him.

We got on the plane, flew the 16-20 hours of the journey, and when we landed in San Francisco and were picked up by our son, we learned that the professor had died that afternoon. The remarkable aspect of this story is that as we drove back to the city from the airport, and I talked on the cell phone to Israel, being apprised of events and planning the next few days, Marilynn sat in the back seat listening, and saying "Reuven has died, we have to go back!" She was passionate and repetitive. Her cogency had come back. She knew how much he loved her, and he was an important part of her awareness. She was never sure why we were back in California, and even at a funeral, sitting in front of the coffin, asked several times "who is in there," and "why are we here," despite of being surrounded by her sister, her cousins, and others whom she knew well. But she kept saying "we have to go back to Israel, Reuven has died!"

We flew back to Israel immediately after the funeral, and for the next week, during the remainder of the mourning period, going to the cemetery, and the memorial events, she was fully cogent, understanding what was going on, being with the family and friends who were participating, and the like. Professor Feuerstein, and our life with him and

our related associates, was so meaningful for her that it sustained her attention. When the events of his passing were completed she returned to her previous state.

We were at the point where I realized that I could no longer be her caregiver, and decided that we would take her back to the US. She did not have any awareness of what was taking place. She had listened to discussions and the planning but it did not register. She saw me packing clothing, sorting out what we will take and what we will leave, as I was planning (hopefully) to return to Israel and our apartment in the foreseeable future. She even sat with me as I described to others our plans for the future, which include her living in a residential care environment. She either did not react, making me wonder what was being registered and understood, or occasionally would make simple comments—"I like that," or "That's what I need." Again I didn't know what she understood.

On a weekend close to the time of our departure we were visiting elderly cousins living on a kibbutz, one of whom is in an elder care residential facility. As we sat talking with her, I was observing Marilynn's awareness or reaction to being there. I didn't discern any. Later when I commented as we took our leave from the family that where our cousin Nettie was living would be good for Marilynn. She heard that and interjected into the conversation that "yes, she would like that." To my great surprise!

THE NEED FOR RESIDENTIAL CARE

Thus we returned to San Francisco. We first had to consider where should we put her in care—Israel or the US. There were financial problems and risks of doing it in Israel. And also the question of home care or in a residential setting, which would be better for her. Another aspect was the kind of life I wanted to lead after Marilynn was placed in care. I had wrestled with the question of placing her in care in Israel or the US. The financial issues of staying in Israel, with its lower costs of providing care, presented logistical problems. Although we were Israeli citizens we had never secured health care or paid income tax. In addition, one needed to get government permission to hire a foreign care worker, the proper health insurance coverage she would need, the effect on my working life (with frequent travel out of the country). I consulted with several financial experts, learned about what it would take to overcome the difficulties, and decided to take her back to California and place her in care there. In this decision I consulted with Alan and David, and together as a family we decided that being in the US, and in California, we could deal with her needs as a family, even if I decided to return to Israel.

Our son Alan searched and found a small residential program for dementia care. There were only 6 or 8 beds, with very personal care, in a family home environment. Since I was hoping to return to Israel, Alan and his family agreed to monitor her care, and so the placement they chose was only a 10 minute drive from their home. During the next almost two years Alan or his family members visited her once a week, and when I was in the Bay Area I would do the same.

Early in the placement we—myself and Alan and his family--visited her weekly, cutting down from every few days. I was going every few days. The care giving staff conveyed to us that these frequent visits seemed to confuse her, and we were told that often she "regressed" for a few hours after these visits. So once a week seemed right, and we continued this frequency until the end, through the several placement settings she lived in. As we visited her, at times she would acknowledge us, toward the end she did not. Sometimes her face would be blank, other times expressive with the old "twinkle" in her eyes. But this is getting ahead of the story as I want to tell it.

When I took her to the placement, on a Sunday afternoon, I expected her to ask where she was and why she was staying there. She did not. When I said to the caregiver that I would stay and help her with dinner I was told that it was not necessary and that they could (and wanted) to handle the situation without me. I returned the next morning, again expecting Marilynn to express some concerns about why she was there, but again nothing. I was concerned that they would have difficulty showering her, as she had become very resistant with me. Again, they said not to worry, they could handle it. Another realization that this was the appropriate move to be made.

When I returned home after leaving her in the care setting, I found myself feeling empty and missing the routines that I had been engaged in for the past 4 or 5 years. Putting to bed, waking up, picking out her clothes and dressing her, toileting, brushing teeth, preparing her breakfast, settling her in front of the TV, going for short walks, etc. What surprised me was that none of that had felt onerous, it was just part of our being together, and I missed not having it. Even though we had not had meaningful conversations for several years, had not slept in the same bed for several years, I had not been lonely. Now I was! And continue to be…in the evenings at home.

For the next year, this was her placement. She was well taken care of, spent most of her days watching television in a day room with the other residents, and was only minimally cognizant of who I was when I visited. I remember asking her who I was and she responded after a pause and searching my face, “My husband.” This was slower and slower to come, and such recognition disappeared entirely. She often would squirm in her chair, and rub her face. It was difficult to tell if she was physically uncomfortable, but the medical consultations we got at that point indicated not.

Earlier in this story, I wrote about our son Alan’s ALS condition. At a certain point when Alan was very debilitated, and the doctors said he would not live much longer, Marilynn’s sister and brother-in-law, and another sister-in-law came to San Francisco to see Alan and Marilynn. Marilynn did not know of Alan's condition. We felt she was past understanding and thus never knew of Alan's situation or his death. During this visit we brought Marilynn to a nearby restaurant to see them, feeling that if we all descended on her in the small care facility it might be overwhelming. So 8 people sat at a table in a quiet corner. Marilynn sat across from her sister, and began to stare at her (a focusing behavior that was not much in evidence in her care facility). After a few minutes she voiced "Sister, sister." She did not say anything else during this encounter.

After approximately a year we began to feel that there was not enough stimulation for her in the small facility. We searched and found a larger facility that had a dementia program that promised more mental stimulation. It was geographically away from Alan's family, but he was already into the physical debilitation of his ALS condition and it was clear that he would no longer be able to monitor his mother's care. And I did not want the burden to fall on his family as they had so much to deal with regarding Alan's condition. The residential placement was close to where I lived in San Francisco, and since I was planning to change my life from living in Israel to returning to reside in San Francisco, the new placement would enable me to monitor her care.

Here our personal savior Judy Delphia re-enters the picture. She had been her caregiver on-demand as I described in the previous chapter. Since she had a professional background in-home health care and treatment of the elderly with dementia (she had previously taken care of my mother, 15 years earlier and in many truly extraordinary ways) she helped us find a more appropriate placement. So at the time of my coming back to live in San Francisco, and search for a hopefully more stimulating environment for Marilynn, Judy helped with the search and we settled on what would be Marilynn's second placement. For a few months, it seemed like a good move, but soon Judy and I began to feel that she was not getting what was promised and that Marilynn was being neglected. They were not taking her to the activities provided for others, not changing her undergarments enough, and when I observed them feeding her while she was lying on a couch instead of getting her up to eat with others at a table, the warning bells started to sound for me. As an experiment, I took Marilynn and a few other dementia res idents and did some simple Feuerstein exercises to stimulate mental processes, and as she and the others started to respond (over two or three 40 minute sessions) I could see the caregivers stare in wonderment. These residents could respond and communicate, rather than sit unattended in front of the television for the entirety of their day. When I shared this with the program administrator, and suggested that I train the caregivers in doing some of the mental activities I got a vague assent but no follow up action. Eventually we (Judy and I) decided to look for another placement.

One of the insights I gained from this experience was to look for a placement that was fully dedicated to what is called "memory care" rather than a placement for which memory care is one of the options. After a more thorough search of the Bay Area, we settled on one relatively close geographically to where I lived. By this time Judy was living in Kansas City, but every few months would come to see Marilynn. At those times she would sit with Marilynn for four to five hours, talking to her, singing to her, and Marilynn would acknowledge her presence. By this time she was not speaking, but would lean toward her and make fleeting eye contact.

The move was the right thing to do. Marilynn's mental state was so regressed that the facility's activity focus was well above her ability to respond. Nonetheless, they got her up every morning, dressed her, she had her meals in the dining room, and then was taken to every activity. If she seemed restless they would take her for walks, and then wheel her in her mobile chair when she could no longer walk. And most importantly, the caregivers showed that they liked her, talked to her, and paid attention to her needs. I later felt that had we found a place like this at the outset she might have held her cogency somewhat longer.

This was her last place of being. I would visit her once a week; sit with her in the dining room or in the room where activity was taking place. I will never know whether she recognized me at that time, or whether she was getting anything from being at the activities. However, there is some evidence from the expanding brain sciences that stimulation may make a difference, whether or not the individual can acknowledge or respond.

THE LOSS OF PHYSICAL CONTACT

Here I return to the subject of physical responding. Recall that earlier in our relationship, when Marilynn was fully functioning, we were very physical and sexual. As she began the palpable deterioration, she began to recoil from touching, as though it was painful. The sexual act was less and less possible. We had always enjoyed touching each other, and hold our bodies close throughout the night as we slept in the same bed. This was no longer possible. She did not want to be touched or held. I respected this and did not want to force myself on her. It was clear that even if passive, sex was no longer stimulating or pleasurable for her. So I stopped.

In bed, she was restless, with movement akin to restless leg syndrome. Another accommodation was necessary. I moved our queen-size bed into another bedroom and got single beds, in a side-by-side configuration with no space in between. This worked for a while until the leg restlessness became so severe that I felt it in my bed next to hers. The next move was to have her sleep in the other bedroom, with the doors open so I could hear if she needed something during the night. That worked—she seemed more restful in her sleep—and became the sleeping format for the rest of our time together. But it ended a very important part of our relationship, the physical closeness that was a central part of our lives together, in bed and without.

MOURNING MY LOSS

Given the long and slow process of Marilynn's dementia, and the various strategies of accommodation and denial that I have already described, I found myself in a mourning process of which I was not fully aware. This occurred several years before her passing. However from the perspective of retrospection, and my background as a psychologist,

I can see more clearly now how my mourning process occurred, often without my conscious awareness. Here I borrow from Elizabeth Kubler-Ross's delineation of stages of reaction to loss due to death—and in my journey with Marilynn into her gradual descent into dementia, there were certain stages. I will go through the Kubler-Ross stages and how I experienced them with Marilynn.

Denial—this isn't happening. My children pointed out long before the florid symptoms appear that their mother was failing mentally. As I look back I can see it, but I did not while it was happening. Even when she would get lost for hours at a time when driving home from the market, and when appearing mysteriously and not having any sense of what had happened or why we were freaked out I didn't connect it to something larger. Before the onset of clear indicators, friends who had not seen her for several years would take me aside and say "what is wrong with Marilynn" and I would only vaguely understand and acknowledge their observations. Now I see that denial as "enabling." For her, making her world functional, with or without awareness. For me, keeping things comfortable, stable, doable.

Accommodation: OK, there are things she cannot do. I will help her, or stop certain actions. When I would no longer let her drive a car, and was able to take her where she needed to go, a problem was solved. That she never understood why I was restricting her, and her anger with me for years afterword I took to be simply her need to be in control. And her arguments as to why and under what conditions she should be allowed to drive I understood as her strong personality and independent spirit. Similarly in the kitchen, as she lost the ability to plan and sequence the cooking and baking activities that she loved, I stopped her and in some cases prevented her doing dinner parties for friends and family, and structured our eating habits to reduce "cooking" demands. Being a "talker" and believing in "relationship transparency" when I explained why we were making these changes she would argue, often saying "You are making me more disabled than I am!" So I stopped confronting and explaining. But I kept re-organizing our lives to reduce the threat and impact of her disabilities. Now, in retrospect, I question whether I was doing it for me or for her. Probably both! Anger:

Why is she doing this to me? She could be responsive, but won't, and damn it, she should. And I would push her—verbally, mentally, and in rare moments of my despair toward the end of my role as primary caregiver, physically. In the early days of her dementia she would strike back, verbally and with her anger. And we would physically separate and then come back to one another with apologies. Later she would simply not understand what had happened and why I was reacting as I was. Fortunately I saw that, and stopped expressing my internalized reactions, which from the advantage of longer-range retrospection caused much internal stress. But I loved her, and even more so, I am a "professional," so I should know and do differently. And the ultimate irony was that since I knew that a few minutes or hours later she would not recall anything of the negative encounters, I felt reprieved of any transgressions, and "we could start over." Eventually the anger recedes and acceptance begins to coalesce.

Acceptance: OK, it is what it is. She cannot help it. It is not her… she—as I know her—is gone. I love her, I will take care of her, I will be a competent caregiver, and my mastery of this role will give me comfort. And so it has been. I watched for the small islands of awareness and enjoyed them. I watched them get smaller and less frequent, and I knew that this was the progression of her disease, out of her control and not the fault of my limitations. I planned for activities that would engage her and have the potential to slow down the progression of her loss. I saw instances of how she could "come back" when she was with family and friends, and gets something from long familiar routines—going to people's homes, out to eat meals, being in airports and traveling to cities she has been in before. This was in the earlier stages of her decline, but these experiences became less and less possible. That was much of our life for the past 25 years, and she was an exited partner in it. But it is what it is, and while from time to time it still breaks my heart to recall her in our shared youth and actively engaged adult lives, I know that what will and is happening is out of our (my) control, and we can truly make the best of it.

Getting On With It: The most difficult thing for me has been to come to awareness and acceptance. Sometimes the awareness comes from unexpected events. When I took her for the first time to an adult day program for elders with dementia, and watched her sit at a table with others and start to participate in the program I saw that she was as disabled as everyone else in the room, perhaps more so. It was a kind of "release." I could see her in the context of others, and I had two reactions: she needs this place, this level of care; and she is disabled, it is not something that is a function of how I deal with her, how I reason with her, what she has control over. I recall walking away with such a strong ambivalence—others must help her, it is not something that I can be responsible for or change, and I must reframe my expectations and efforts. But with tears in my eyes nonetheless!

7

Finding A New Life

San Francisco-Los Angeles
2016-Present

This chapter will be considerably shorter than those that preceded it, for this book is meant to be primarily about Marilynn and not me! It describes the last two years of my life (worry not, I am still alive and writing!). Marilynn and I had more than 50 years together, and I have embarked on this part of the journey for not quite two years. How I arrived at this "new life" is connected and influenced by my life with Marilynn. This should fill out the story of Marilynn and my relationship, but since this is meant to be primarily the story of Marilynn I will be succinct. Again I owe a debt to Barry Peterson, but more of that a little bit farther along. At the outset, I must reveal that I was not someone who believed that "fate" determined the courses of our lives. But the events described in this chapter have challenged this belief and are changing my sense of the processes of life, for reasons that will become clear!

THE EXPERIENCE OF LONELINESS

After placing Marilynn in residential care in the San Francisco area, and making very comfortable arrangements at the outset, I returned to Israel to continue my work. But it was difficult. I had a vague sense of disquiet, and it affected my concentration. It was hard to be in the apartment without her, even thinking about the more difficult times caring for her. The routines were different. I was surrounded by the objects of our 15 years of enjoying our home environment, and even being at the Institute without her sitting across from me in my office and interacting with all of our colleagues and friends seemed missing.

I found myself being in settings where the atmosphere was upbeat and happy, watching the families and couples interacting, and feeling a sense of sadness. I began to watch people on the streets, couples walking hand in hand, and thinking that I had had that and wondering whether would I ever experience the joy of companionship again. Even some of my existential optimism began to erode. I stopped taking care of myself, I ate more junk food, found myself constantly snacking—all quite contrary to my previous life routines.

Then I was given Barry Peterson's book about his life with Jan that I described in an earlier chapter. His narrative, open and heartfelt, encouraged me to seek companionship. That it was OK to think about a future and that it was not being disloyal to my memory of Marilynn, even though she was still alive. I could love someone new, if I were fortunate enough to find someone, and not diminish my love of Marilynn! So I began to think about what I wanted and needed, and I was able to place it into the context of the very good life that Marilynn and I had. In the last two years of being in Israel with Marilynn, before we decided to place her in care in the US, I had a great deal of time to do this thinking, primarily as I sat in the evening on our apartment balcony after putting her to bed, usually before 7:00 PM.

At the same time, I was becoming disillusioned with my work at the Institute. In retrospect, I see much of that, but not all, as a consequence of my depression, that I did not acknowledge. If I had found a meaningful partner in Israel perhaps my "new life" might have taken a very different course. In any event, after two years following my return, I decided it was time to "retire" from the Institute and go back to San Francisco and start to build a new life. Marilynn was in residential care in the Bay Area, my beloved mentor Professor Feuerstein had passed away (several years earlier), and I had lost much of my enthusiasm for the work, something that concerned me greatly. I did not know what it would be like to return home after several decades of living in Israel, but I felt I had to make a change.

BEGINNING THE SEARCH

So I began a search, first in Israel, and then when I returned to the US. Before returning I met a few women in Israel, but it was more of a casual search. Nothing was promising, but maybe I was not quite ready yet. Then back in the US, I joined one of the computer dating services. I filled out the profiles, began to see possible matches, and even made follow-up contacts with a few likely prospects. But I greatly disliked the process. It seemed so shallow and superficial. How do I present myself, given my "advanced" age and relatively limited social life and needs? I was not into what seemed like the modern modalities of social life, even for those of us at an advanced age. I had never been into the bar scene and the social drinking; I was not interested in clubs or rock concerts. But even with these seeming limitations, and played the game, I even physically met one woman for a casual meeting rather than a date, and came away extremely unsatisfied. The rest of the descriptions of potential matches were unappealing.

Around this time I noticed a small advertisement in a Jewish newspaper (I am Jewish, but not particularly observant) for a "Jewish Matchmaker." I called her to find out the details, what it cost and what the logistics would be. In the course of the conversation, she asked me to describe myself and what my life was like. When I told her that I had spent a major part of the past 25 years in Israel, working with Professor Reuven Feuerstein, she gasped and said "I know Reuven! I lived in Israel and did my national service requirement working in his Institute." We spent the rest of the conversation talking about our mutual experiences with him. One of the first in a string of "coincidences" that conspired to challenge my rejection of "fate."

I stopped computer dating and engaged my Jewish matchmaker. She interviewed me comprehensively to get a picture of who would be a good match—a retired professor, a psychologist, background in Israel, Jewish but not observant, lover of dogs, and—importantly—someone who had experienced a very long time positive marital relationship. She did her job well. Through her, I met 5 or 6 women in the Bay Area, and they mostly met the criteria I had conveyed. But none of them excited me and led me to want further contacts. Was I still being resistant? And I felt very awkward with the whole process. One criterion, that I am less proud of but knew I needed to establish was that I wanted someone who was youthful in appearance and would bring me back to a level of physical intimacy that was lost to me as Marilynn faded away.

The matchmaker asked me if I would consider someone outside the Bay Area and I said OK. She gave me the name of a woman in San Diego, I called her, and we agreed to meet. It was February and I was getting ready to make a motor trip to the Midwest for two months of consulting and teaching and decided I could swing south to San Diego to see her before heading east. It helps that I greatly enjoy long-distance driving.

While this was ensuing, and I was at a conference in Mexico, I received a call from the matchmaker. She told me that she had another candidate, living in Los Angeles, and this woman would be a wonderful match for me. I said OK, send me her information, and I would contact her when I returned from my two-month engagement. She encouraged me, suggesting that I stop in LA on my way south, and not wait to meet her. I agreed, gave myself an extra day, and followed through.

WERE THINGS "MEANT TO HAPPEN?"

I met Vera in a restaurant; a few blocks from her office in Santa Monica. She is a practicing psychologist with a full and active practice. I followed the matchmaker's advice on such first meetings. Don't get too personal, don't have a meal, talk generally, and decide whether you want another meeting. If so, you can arrange it or the matchmaker will intervene for you.

My recollections of that first meeting were that we had a lot to talk about...our shared experiences as psychologists, our dogs, a bit about our families. She recalls that when I spoke of Marilynn and my life with her (even though I thought I was staying away from emotional details) I had tears in my eyes. She remembers that as an endearing quality. I recall that she met my general physical requirements, she was

small and slim and did not look her age, which is five years young than I. But I also do not look my age physically. But I didn't say to myself at the time "boy she is beautiful." Now I think that she is physically exquisite.

Part of the above reaction was due to my impending long journey, part to my anticipation of meeting another woman the next day, but a big part was a caution conveyed to me by my son David. Just before this experience, as he had correctly assessed my need system in this whole "dating process," had said to me "Dad, be careful. Don't put too much into these prospective relationships. Don't expect the same sense of family and commitment you had with your mother. She was special and you can have a nice relationship with another woman without having what you had with mother." After two years of being with Vera, I'm glad that he was wrong. But with anyone else he might have been correct, but it wouldn't have met my needs.

When Vera and I parted I asked her if she would like to stay in contact and she said yes. I told her I would call her from time to time from my midwestern journey and send her emails. She said that she was not a good e-mailer. But within a day or two, she sent me an email telling me that she enjoyed our meeting. Over the next two months, I called her several times. Her recollection is that I did not call her much, and she might have been right as I was deeply engaged in my activities, didn't at the time feel a sense of commitment and that in my son David's eyes, was not a "great communicator." But events conspired to transform interest, into affection and commitment.

When I returned to California, I called her and we set up a "date." There followed three more dates that I arranged by coming to Los Angeles. We had dinner, went to museums, went for walks, and got to know each other. The first date was in a restaurant across the street from a building where I had spent 15 years working as a consultant. Another sign of the conspiring of fate? I was still uncertain and careful, remembering David's admonitions. Throughout our dating, she invited me to a family Passover seder, to a Mother's Day celebration with her family, both of which I declined. On the third date, I decided to discuss my physical needs, what I wanted from a relationship, and she told me that she felt the same way. I began to think of her differently, and focus on her physical qualities

FROM CONNECTION TO COMMITTMENT

"Getting to know one another" further challenged my sense of the power of the fates. Vera had lost her husband, a professor of medicine and highly esteemed medical practitioner, four years earlier to the same rare variant of ALS that took my son Alan. As she described her care giving efforts with him, and I described my life with Marilynn's descent into dementia, we felt we had had deeply shared experiences. Moreover, she described a loving 45- year marriage, parenting two children, with close extended family ties and support. It was almost fully consonant with my marriage, parenting, and family experiences. It began to feel that we had two very similar life scripts.

And the last major blow of fate: when I was still ruminating about what I wanted, she invited me to join her in Long Beach while she attended a weekend professional conference. I initially said no. It was a time when I was undergoing surgery for testicular cancer, which turned out to be fully successful, and I have been in remission ever since. But I had spent a lonely weekend in San Francisco, even though I had met with friends. So I said to myself "Maybe I should go down. What do I have to lose? Another weekend of sitting around feeling down? Why not?" It also meant staying in the hotel with her, a commitment that frightened me. I had not been with another woman in 50 years, had just had testicular surgery, and had not been sexually active with Marilynn for 5 or 6 years. Scary, but I did it!

I came down on a Friday morning, sat with her in one of her seminars, and prepared for an "adventure." After the first night, which turned out wonderfully, we went for a long walk, the first of what has become one of the signature activities in our new life together. During that first three-hour walk we shared personal intimacies of our lives, and I recall telling her things that I never thought I would share with another human being. At the end of that walk, I knew that she was the one for me, and I wanted to spend the rest of my life with her (excuse my romanticism). We did a few more walks, had meals together, and talked and talked. On Sunday morning I had to return to San Francisco for an early medical appointment the next morning. As I sat waiting for the flight I got a phone call from Marilynn's sister, with whom I had a very close relationship. As I described my weekend with Vera I felt myself choked up with emotion as I described my newly forming feelings for this woman. It was so strong emotionally that I could hardly talk. That surprised me but I realized that what had just happened for me was something very special. With that insight, I had to call David, even though it was early morning and he's a late sleeper, feeling I had to share my experience with him and got choked up again. It was real and powerful. I felt changed, excited, and ready for a new life. Much later when I told Vera about this experience in the airport she told me that as soon as she got home she called her son and daughter and expressed much the same thing.

How did I know? We each shared how much we loved our spouses, what our lives had been like, and the difficulties for us as we experienced taking care of them and our loss. Although Marilynn was still alive at the time, she had been emotionally gone for me for close to five years. We both were ready to move on into new lives, without diminishing our loving memories of our pasts. We understood and empathized with one another.

A NEW LIFE EMERGES AND SOLIDIFIES

As our lives together have unfolded and developed, we continue to talk about her David and my Marilynn, and we draw strength and understanding from this. We were ready and it felt right. And after two years of being together, we feel we know one another's experience, and it brings a sense of continuity to our relationship. I keep a picture of her David on my desk as I work, and often look at it and say a silent "thank you" for giving her to me. My son David and her children accept and take pleasure in the happiness we bring to one another. We share family experiences in a warm extended family, on special holidays and just ordinary encounters. And for all of us, my Marilynn and Vera's David are never far from our consciousness, in ways that strengthen our insight into our relationship. She brings to me the strengths, values, family connections from her positive 45 years with her David. And I believe I do the same for her.

Thus we go on into the rest of our lives. My life with Marilynn will always contribute to our happiness and comfort, as will Vera's David.

EPILOGUE

How did all this come to pass? I am not a "believer," in the theological sense of the term. If anything, I am more of an existentialist, and the secular mold of Sartre. I have always seen the concept of God as a hypothetical construct, developed by sentient human beings to explain and make meaningful observations of the world around them, in the absence of scientific knowledge. Not to disparage their conclusions, but rather to see them as rational, thoughtful reactions to the existential issues of life. Faith is important, but faith in what— god or the scientific discoveries affecting aspects of life, and death? Even in the most stressful times of my life with Marilynn, as the regression moved toward the totality of her being, and affected my relationship with her, I continued to see it from my scientific/rational perspective. It was happening and I would deal with it!

Two factors started to change my thinking and feeling. One was my long association with Reuven Feuerstein, a deeply religious and thoughtful man, from whom I learned a great deal about the Judaism I grew up with. He was always the teacher, respecting my views, but challenging me to consider the theological possibilities (that are a central aspect of religious/observant Judaism). Being with Reuven was the end of a long journey of study and career with mentors who seemed to "guide" me toward formative experience with this remarkable man (who knew and had interacted with all of my previous mentors, from the beginning of my student days and career). The second has been my relationship with my Vera, who deeply believes in god. Whenever I express my feeling of being lucky and blessed (in the non-religious sense) she adamantly counters with "No, Lou, only God could have brought us together!" And given my devotion to her, how can I argue? I am fully not there yet, but my being with Vera may well change me.

As of April of 2019 Marilynn became of "of blessed memory." Her suffering had ended. After two years of almost complete deterioration, not being able to recognize her surroundings and communicate any awareness, observing her writhing in her chair, eyes closed most of the time, unable to maintain any physical posture without support, with the affirmation of her caregivers, my son and I with the support of her caregivers mutually agreed that her situation prompted a referral to hospice. The hospice nurses assessed her and concluded that she was in pain, but could not communicate it, or have it alleviated.

My son David and I agreed that it was time to end her suffering, and we agreed to heavily sedate her, and allow her to stay in her bed and not get her up for meals or activities. When we saw her for the first time in her sedated state, resting calmly with her eyes closed, a certain sadness and tension lifted, especially for David. It was the first time in several years that he did not leave her presence without tears in his eyes.

The care facility in which she resided agreed and complied with the "end of life" protocol that was prescribed and monitored by Hospice. In California, if a patient in care indicates a readiness to take food they must be fed. Marilynn responded positively when she was approached. She had been on a liquid diet before the sedation, due to aspiration issues. She had lost considerable weight and appeared almost skeletal. So for a week or so into the sedation regimen, she accepted nourishment, and then she stopped responding. We knew the end was in sight. I had a long-planned trip abroad scheduled, and David and I agreed that I should go and he would deal with the situation when and if she died which we estimated would be a week to 10 days. I was planning to be away for two weeks. I travelled on a Friday, and the following Tuesday she passed away.

As I write this I try to summarize what my life with Marilynn was like, especially in the later years. For at least a decade at the outset of her descent, I did the things I always did, we calibrated our lives accordingly, and not until almost the very end, did I become aware of how I had sustained—in this regard I hope in the most positive of ways—her and our comfortable and productive lives together. In this last period, when I came to the understanding that I could no longer be her primary caregiver, I opened myself to what family and friends had observed and been telling me for several years—that my wife and companion, David and Alan's mother, Marilynn, this person who I loved and wanted to be with, in daily life, in adventurous travel throughout the world, was in fact, limited and growing more so and would never recover.

As I further thought about the progression, I guess you had to have some distance in time and space to see it. I acknowledged that friends and colleagues, who saw her—often over time—and with whom she interacted, would tell me of their observations. I think I was almost blinded regarding her functioning about the effects of how I was helping and supporting her, and how these actions had made her able to function, participate, and be part of a wider and meaningful world. But in retrospect I am glad that this had been our life together. I will always cherish it. And from an even farther away perspective, I have been told by several who knew and observed us that they could see what I was doing and they respected it. I was often called a "hero." This was a designation that I felt very uncomfortable with at the time. Now it is comforting and confirming.

One more aspect to this insight: I now know that what I did was not just for her. It was self-serving. It was for me! We were two parts of a whole. Perhaps I did not fully appreciate it at the time. But in the six or seven years since she started her decline, I have come to better understand it. Maybe not fully, because it is still coming, and I suspect it will for the remainder of my life (with the help of my loving partner Vera, who shares in the recounting of this story and helps me understand it).

If I have any regrets now it is that while Marilynn and I were together, through our long relationship, I did not as fully appreciate Marilynn's strength, beauty, and the role she played in my life as I do now. Yet from this vantage point, even with the difficult aspects of her dementia, I am grateful for our experience together. I only wish I had more overtly conveyed this to her as our lives unfolded.

Lastly, as I conclude the writing of this memoir my memories of her are strengthened, and some of the sadness of her loss has returned, but I feel more complete. In the Jewish tradition when the name of a departed loved one is mentioned it is followed by the phrase "of blessed memory." And for me Marilynn is! I am content with the feeling that… "it is better to have loved and lost than to not haved loved at all"

POSTSCRIPT

For those of you who have read this book and have had the experience of living with the dementia of a loved one, similar to mine with Marilynn or differently, you may be wondering, as did I (even with my background as a mental health professional), what are the technical details of the disorder and how to understand them.

It is difficult, as the disorders of dementia are hard to diagnose, and the signs of the disorder exhibit a range of severity and time of onset. Another factor is that neurosciences are developing so rapidly that knowledge of neural disorders is changing rapidly. When my son was diagnosed with ALS, the neurologist dissuaded me from going online to learn about it because, in his view, the knowledge base was developing so rapidly that I was likely to get a good deal of misinformation.

In this postscript my objective is to briefly review what is known, at the time of this writing, about the disorders that I describe in this book relating to Marilynn's decline into dementia, and broaden it out so as to be of relevance to a wider range of experience, but still within the boundaries of the book's narrative. It is particularly relevant because it was never established exactly what Marilynn had, and what the causes were. I describe this situation in the book.

The term dementia comprises various disorders and is caused by diverse factors, some of which are amenable to treatment and "curing," but most not. The disorder may be slow developing or of rapid onset. Marilynn's was slow developing. The most accurate generalization that can be made is that dementia, of whatever cause or symptomatic format, is a neurodegenerative disorder. This term denotes progressive loss of neurons, from different regions of the brain, thus determining the various forms and degrees of dementia. The differential speed of the degeneration is what determines the rapidity of the course of the disease.

The most commonly identified (and diagnosed) types of disorders are Alzheimer's disease, Frontal Temporal Disorder (FTD), and

Lewy body dementia. Less common but relatively well-known is ALS (amyotrophic lateral sclerosis). There are variants within these disorders, and they can be mixed, meaning that a given form of dementia can have symptoms of more than one causative condition at the same time.

One of the more difficult things to tease out in the process of diagnosis is the cause and effect of cognitive impairment, either due to one of the disease entities noted above, or as a result of vascular contributions to deficient cognitive functioning. This requires a process of differential diagnosis, with difficulty determining what the behavioral indicators mean (sometimes in the field of diagnosis referred to as soft signs).

The National Institute of Aging identifies a number of conditions that present symptoms of cognitive dysfunction that are difficult to differentiate from neurologically based diseases. They indicate those whose behaviors resemble dementia:

- Side effects of medications
- Emotional stress
- Vitamin deficiencies
- Alcoholism
- Vascular incidents including strokes, blood clots, tumors, brain infections
- Traumatic head injury
- Thyroid and other endocrinological conditions

The process of diagnosing involves taking a history, doing a physical examination, administering neurological tests, and brain scans such at CT, MRI, PET (that are termed "non-invasive" methods of observing brain functioning in real-time, that is while the individual is functioning and alert, so named because they do not require any surgical interventions), and through genetic studies. This last method is relatively new, and is tracing newly identified causes of the neurodegenerative conditions.

The symptoms of dementia are also diverse, and overlap the diagnosed entities, making differentiation of the disease difficult. Among them are

- Memory loss: for procedures such as using the telephone, computing change in financial transactions, finding the way home, as examples.

- Asking the same questions repeatedly.

- Getting lost in known environments.

- Not being able to follow directions.

- Confusion regarding time, place, and people.

- Not taking care of oneself, with regard to personal hygiene, eating, dressing and undressing, and the like.

Differentiating Dementia

Alzheimer's disease comprises 60-80% of the diagnosed condition of dementia. Researchers have identified 50 additional causes of dementia. Some symptoms improve with treatment but most do not, hence the condition is generally considered progressive. The various forms of dementia can be classified into:

- Degenerative neurological diseases: Alzheimer' disease, Parkinson's disease, Huntington's disease, and some types of Muscular Sclerosis.

- Vascular disorders: strokes, blood clots, etc.

- Traumatic brain injury

- Infections of the nervous system: meningitis, HIV

- Types of hydrocephalus: accumulation of fluid on the brain

Another differentiation is where in the brain does the degeneration occurs. It can occur cortically, meaning in the cerebral cortex that is the outer layer of the brain. Cortical disorders usually involve severe memory and language loss, such as in Alzheimer's disease. The degeneration can also be subcortical, with little or no memory loss, but dysfunctions in initiating action, speed of reaction, and motor movement. Examples of disorders that are subcortical are Parkinson's and Huntington's diseases, and HIV. In some instances, degeneration can be both cortical and subcortical.

With regard to Marilynn's dementia, I will provide more details on two of the diseases that most likely contributed to her dementia:
Frontal Temporal Disorder (FTD): This disorder involved progressive degeneration of the frontal and temporal lobes of the brain. These are the parts of the brain that process information and initiate cognitive responses. In the population of individuals under the age of 60 it is the most commonly diagnosed form of dementia. It is often initially misdiagnosed as Alzheimer's or Parkinson's diseases or vascular dementia, as was the case with Marilynn. Further diagnosis and observation frequently clarifies the diagnosis, although in many instances a clear differentiation is never established, again as was the situation with Marilynn.

FTD is observed in three variants:

- A behavioral variant: where behavior changes are the primary observable characteristic.

- A somatic variant: where changes in bodily functions are observed.

- A non-fluent/agrammatic variant: where the disorder primarily is manifested in language functioning, such as in a progressive aphasia (the inability to initiate or respond linguistically.

It is also indicated that a small number of the population also develop FTD with ALS. That appeared to be the case with my son Alan, who is also mentioned in the book.

Summarizing the effects of FTD, we observe gradual but steady changes in behavior, language functioning, and a slowness or weakness of movement.

ALS: This condition is primarily a motor neuronal degenerative condition in adults, onset within the age range of 40-70. It is 20% more common in men. The primary degeneration is in motor functioning, although there is also cognitive deficit in approximately 20% of those diagnosed (the FTD variant). The motor degeneration is in muscular functioning, affecting body movement and speech production. Statistically, those diagnosed with ALS live 3-5 years post diagnosis, although there are exceptions, such as Stephen Hawking.

As indicated at the outset, this is a brief introduction to the nature of dementia. There is extensive information, easily accessible, through the on-line resources of the Internet. Such information goes well beyond what is presented here, and will more clearly define what you have observed in your interactions with your loving companions, as occurred for me with my Marilynn.

CPSIA information can be obtained
at www.ICGtesting.com
Printed in the USA
LVHW111041081122
732584LV00003BA/124

9 781959 071228